The Gates of Prayer

The Gates of Prayer
Twelve Talks on Davvenology

Rabbi Zalman Schachter-Shalomi
Boulder, Colorado, June 2010

With contributions by
Michael Kosacoff

Edited by
N.M-Y.

Albion
Andalus
The Jewish Renewal Series
Boulder, CO
2011

"The old shall be renewed,

and the new shall be made holy."

— Rabbi Avraham Yitzhak Kook

Albion-Andalus, Inc.
P. O. Box 19852
Boulder, CO 80308
www.albion-andalus.com

Design and composition by Albion-Andalus, Inc.

Cover design by Daryl McCool, D.A.M. Cool Graphics

Cover illustration: An oil painting of the Altneushul in Prague by C. Grueb, 1876.

Manufactured in the United States of America

ISBN-10: 1456505203

ISBN-13: 978-1456505202

In Memoriam

L'illuy Nishmot of Beynush Dobbs, Esther bat Shmuel Ekus, Moshe ben R'uben Foster, Rabbi Chayah Rachel Levine, Rabbi Aryeh Hirschfield, Paul Podwin, and Cantor Susan Wehle, whose memories are a blessing.

Contents

Acknowledgments

I wish to thank Michael Kosacoff for all of his help in putting this series of talks together, for discussing the material with me, and for reading the manuscript; to Mary Fulton, my secretary for transcribing the original material and doing the initial editing; and to my student, Netanel Miles-Yepez for doing the final editing and annotation.

Preface

When I was studying in the Lubavitcher *yeshivah,* one evening, some of the older Hasidim sat down together around a table with some vodka and fruit and were having a *farbrengen.* During their conversation, Rabbi Shmuel Levitin, one of my *mashpiyyim,* spoke up in Yiddish complaining that the younger students at the *yeshivah* were not properly involved in deep prayer.

When I heard him say this, I also took some schnapps, a whole tumbler full, and said, *"L'Hayyim!"* and drank it all down. Then I turned to him and said, "How could you blame us for not going deep into contemplative prayer when you have never shared with us what goes on inside of *you* when you pray?"

Immediately, he took umbrage at this, saying, "How dare you ask such a question?" and then 'chewed me out.'

But I took courage and, using the traditional formula, said, "It's a teaching, and I need to learn it."

He then turned to Rabbi Yisroel Jacobson, my other *mashpiyya,* and said, "He's one of your boys; you tell him." Well, Rabbi Jacobson began to mumble and sputter as he often did, saying, "I have worked on my prayer all my life, and you expect me to tell it to you standing on one leg?"

Then Rabbi Avraham Pariz spoke up and said: "You know, he's right. He needs to hear about what goes on inside."

So Reb Shmuel and Reb Yisroel turned to him and said, "So you to tell him." Reb Avraham took a big tumbler-full of schnapps and drank it down and said, *"L'Hayyim!"* Then he went inside himself and delivered an inner commentary on the traditional morning prayer and took us into his own inner world of sacred enchantment. But when he came to the threshold of the silent Amidah, he said, "From here on is a private matter between God and me."

Can you understand how deeply this touched me?

When people ask me to repeat what Reb Avraham said, I have to confess that I cannot repeat his words. I so internalized them at that time that they have now become integral to my own prayer. The best I can do is share with you some of what I have learned in my own life about deep prayer, for which, what I learned that evening is the foundation. What you are about to read is my own telling of some of the things that are happening to me when I am involved in prayer before the living God.

This book contains the edited transcripts of a video series on davvenology which I delivered in June of 2010. Being based on the transcripts of oral teaching, the structure and content of this book is somewhat less formal than ordinary books. Obviously, my approach with this is not academic, but practical. Therefore, you will not find any serious footnotes or academic explanations. As you read it, I hope you will transport yourself in your imagination to the time and place in which I originally delivered the material. Indeed, this book has been produced for those who may not see the video series at all, as well as to be an aid to those who have watched the video series, but who wish to study the material in written form also. You may likewise find it helpful to consult my book on prayer and meditation in the Jewish tradition called, *Gate to the Heart*. Between these two books, you'll have some fairly solid guidance for your inner life.

— Rabbi Zalman Schachter-Shalomi
The 12th of Tammuz 5770/2010

The birthday and the liberation day of my Rebbe, Yosef Yitzhak Schneersohn, the sixth Lubavitcher Rebbe.

First Talk
An Introduction to Davvenology

Yesterday was the birthday of the Ba'al Shem Tov and Reb Shneur Zalman of Liadi, and that still fills me with a good, good feeling.*

About 300 years ago, people still knew a lot about the form of prayer, but they didn't know much about the content and feeling of it. The Ba'al Shem Tov gave that back to them. He's the one who brought us to a place where we could become re-enchanted. What does that mean? It means that even at this moment, this talk, "this call," as it were, "is being monitored for quality purposes." I truly feel — *shiviti Ha'Shem le negdi tamid* — that I am in God's presence, right now.**

So I need to share with you some of the good things you can find in Jewish spirituality, because I take it that the reason you've come to listen is because you want to have a closer relationship with God. As in the hymn, "Just a closer walk with thee," people really feel 'out of touch.' We don't have the same sense that we used to have about our own direct access to invisible support. That's what we need; but how do we get there?

At this point, we are dealing with having to carve-out inner space. What we're looking for is not 'up there' or 'out there,' despite the language of the past that always spoke of God as "up there," "out there," way beyond. It is much truer for us to find God within, to go right inside. Every one of us has a little space we go to. We go

---

* Rabbi Yisrael ben Eliezer (1698-1760), the Ba'al Shem Tov, was the founder of Hasidism. Rabbi Shneur Zalman of Liadi (1745-1812), the Alter Rebbe, was the founder of the HaBaD lineage of Hasidism.

** Psalms 16:8: "I have set *Y-H-V-H* before me always."

there when we are sad, when we feel lonely, when we need to lick our wounds. It's a space that we normally don't want to show other people. We are the most vulnerable beings when it comes to that space. But that is also the space where we can create a sanctuary for God.

That space shouldn't be narrow and small. We can enlarge it, and everything that we do to enlarge that space will give us wider access — not only to ourselves, to our little ego — but to a much larger place. That is the door. God is much closer to us *there* than if you went to the end of all the galaxies, to the end of the Cosmos to find God. The in-dwelling place is inside, and part of what we will learn is how to make use of that, and to create the inner 'furnishings' that you need to have in order to be able to do the contemplative work, the work of being intimately in-touch with God.

Without creating that space inside, the heart can't begin to feel what it needs to feel. The reason why so many people have felt that the mere recital of Hebrew in the synagogue is not the way to talk with God is because it is not *heart-ful*. When is it that you feel open, vulnerable, loving, intimate, and close? I even want to say, 'cozy.' When I think of the way people in Europe used to say: *Oy! Ribbono shel Olam, Gottinyu, Gottinyu,* which means 'little God.' It doesn't mean that God was little, but they used the diminutive that you use when you love someone. If you love someone named Yankel, you call him Yankele; Hayyim becomes Hayyim'l. So as *tatte* became *tattinyu, Got* became *Gottinyu,* because they wanted to express the closeness they had with God. That is not something that you learn about in theology and philosophy. That is what you get when you make heart-space, and you open it up and bring your contemplative mind into it.

An Inward Journey

Let me show you something that may be helpful to you throughout these talks:

Imagine there is a place, right where the fontanelle suture is in a child, in the baby it is the 'soft spot.' That is where we place the head *t'fillin*. In the back, we have the occipital bone. Now, imagine a line in your skull that goes from the front to the back, and imagine another line that goes from temple to temple. See the place where they intersect.

If you have done that, then you can place yourself away from the front of your face and into that space where the intersection occurs. It's amazing when you look from there to your face, and you begin to see what you show to the world; the outer face isn't quite what is on the inside. It's like the man behind the great mask in *The Wizard of Oz*. You show that on the outside, but on the inside, there's a little man pressing the buttons and pulling the switches.

If you allow yourself now to go down from that space into the heart, and you breathe into that heart-space, you can place yourself there more deeply. In that space, you allow yourself, for a little while, to feel the longing. If you want to do anything spiritual, the motive-power for your spiritual work is the longing: the longing for the 'light,' the longing for 'God,' the longing for 'truth.'

Now, exhale deeply.

If you feel something, mark that place in your feelings so you can return to it later. For much of what we will be doing will be in *that* space within us.

As you breathe out, slowly come back to that place in the center of your skull. And as you breathe out again, come into your face and open your eyes.

Look around and know that you have already under-taken an important journey. It is the journey from the ego to the Self that happens in that place. Once you have felt that, no one can take it away from you. No matter where you are—even the waiting room at the doctor's office—you can go right into that place and find a friend there.

The Sufis like to say that God is their "friend." When we say it in Hebrew, *El melekh n'eman*, it means, 'God, Prince, most loyal friend.' It is a lot better than always having to speak to 'the king.' To speak to the king, I have to get dressed-up and mind my manners; but to my friend, I can *kvetch* if I need to, and I can share the joys that I have that I wouldn't tell anybody else.

I'll give you an example: sometimes, there is a par-ticular moment in taking a lick of an ice cream cone—when you are deeply enjoying it—and you want to be able to say: "You know God, You gave me these taste buds, and I want you to know how much I like this ice cream through them." Do you get the idea? This is a whole other way of doing spirituality. It's not way 'up there,' 'out there.' It's a lot more in the body. The heart needs to begin to feel.

Now, what about the *siddur*? I want to say that the *siddur* needs 'cooking.' I like to describe the liturgy as 'freeze-dried prayer.' What do I mean by that? You read the words; but who wrote the words? Someone who cop-ied down what the person who experienced that experi-ence, expressed.

Imagine King David: He has been suffering all kinds of things—he is in and out of trouble—nevertheless, he's always been taken care of. So he says, "The LORD is my shepherd; I shall not want."* Meaning, I tell myself I shall not experience any privation. I want, and keep on want-ing, all the time, but I will not experience privation.

---

* Psalms 23:1.

Now take a look at what happens. He has the experience. Then he comes and sits with his buddies and they see how he is enjoying his dinner after he has come back from some kind of a foray to bring some food in for the people. Then, as he leans back, they hand him the lyre. They know that he is going to sing now. He begins to sing, "The LORD is my shepherd; I shall not want." (That is the well-known King James Version. I like my own version better, but I'll use this one for its familiarity right now.) "He maketh me to lie down in green pastures." That's very nice, but the Hebrew says, *yarbitzeini*, "He makes me *sprawl* in the grass," which is more real.

In time, it gets written down and then, some years later, someone says, "Here, I found another song of King David." Then they engrave it in tablets or write it on parchment. And through the years, it's been going from Hebrew to Aramaic, to Greek, to Latin, to German, and into English. And through this manufacturing process — both translation and simply setting-it-down in writing — many of wonderfully vital elements were taken out, and what is left over in the black-and-white print on paper is what I call 'freeze-dried experience.'

So what are you going to do with that freeze-dried experience? No wonder it doesn't taste good. Imagine you're hungry, you come and visit me, and I give you freeze-dried or dehydrated soup, and I say, "Eat." And you ask, "Why don't you put a little hot water in it?" Well, feelings are the hot water that you have to put into the *siddur*. So all prayer that is devoid of feeling, feels unanswered, because it wasn't really asked. King David says, "My heart says it is for *You* that I'm looking," . . . "it is after You that I'm looking." If the heart hasn't said that, I don't feel that it's gotten to God's heart to be answered. That's a very important part of this then, to get into the heart.

Learning to Pray

Now take a look. You have your chronological age, but I would bet that your emotional age isn't quite up to your chronological age. I'm not saying only yours; mine is the same way. We are much younger emotionally than chronologically. If I were to ask, "How old are you spiritually?" Well, if you were to then add up all the time you have really spent on spiritual pursuits, would you even get a whole year out of that? Do you see what I'm saying? This is very important: to be able to know what are the skills that we have to use. We learn how to walk quite early. We learn how to talk early, but we can't learn how to pray from books.

There was a great *tzaddik* named Rabbi Abraham Yehoshua Heschel — an ancestor of professor Abraham Joshua Heschel — who said, "If you want to learn how to pray, you have to learn with a praying person."* Why is that? Because it isn't merely a verbal thing.

Nowadays, sociologists and psychologists are saying that we have 'mirror neurons.' So, even as I'm speaking with you, something is happening between us, and my mirror neurons and yours somehow meeting in non-local space. There is an attunement going on. Without that attunement, you can't 'cook' the *siddur*. The heart has to get to the place where it *feels* along with, and is connected to another person who is actually *feeling* something in prayer; that is what happens when you *davven* with real davveners.

Moreover, just as you learn how to read and write, there are certain skills in *kavvanah*. One of the skills has to do with mind-steering (and we will talk about these things at greater length as we go on). Just as no one would expect to take up a violin and be able to play Mendelssohn on it without practice, so it is also with steering

---

* Rabbi Avraham Yehoshua Heschel of Apt (1755-1825) was the founder of the great Heschel dynasty of Hasidism. His direct descendant and namesake was the Jewish philosopher, Rabbi Dr. Abraham Joshua Heschel (1907-1972).

steering your way though prayer and meditation. It takes a certain kind of skill. The body has to learn how to want to do that.

If we could actually see the range of possibility in our vibratory consciousness, we would be amazed; but most of the time, we only have a very narrow range in which we operate. For instance, if I put myself in the 'shopping mall mentality,' my awareness will be confined to a narrow range of objects and prices. But when I think about a poem, I'm now in the *imaginal-affective-emotional* range, getting to the *feel* the metaphor. When I go to a still more *spiritual* level, I go to a much higher level of the vibratory scale. Most people say: "Oh, I can't go so high. I never feel anything there." That's only because they haven't learned to stretch in that direction. The tools that we're going to be learning here will stretch us into much higher levels of vibration where it is possible to be in touch with what we call 'spirit.'

The Tool-Kit

Now, all these things that we're going to be learning are going to become part of your 'tool chest.' You will need to begin to do your inner work, your practice. I can offer instruction, but without practice, the instruction won't help. If you find something I say here instructional, then go inside of yourself and try it out. Perhaps then you'll say, *"Ah, now I get it!"* And each time you *get it*, the getting is not only in your awareness, but also in your body. If you can put the markers of feeling into your body, it's very good.

Reb Nahman of Bratzlav said, "Of every spiritual thing that you learn, you also have to teach it to your body."* Why? Because awarenesses in the mind evaporates so quickly. We have so many theophanies, so many

---

* Rabbi Nahman of Bratzlav (1772-1810) was the founder of the Bratzlav lineage of Hasidism.

holy insights. Where are they now? If I had actually done something with all the insights that I've had in my lifetime, how enlightened I would be now? How much closer would I be to God? The problem is, they disappear; so we have to put them into a vessel that will allow us to recall them. The best vessel of recollection is the 'taste' of them as experienced in our bodies. So we need to learn how to do that.

One of the best ways to prepare for learning is to pray. But first, you have to put yourself in the presence of God (as one does when singing a *niggun*). You know, most people talk *about* God in the third person, as if God were not here, now. Imagine if I were to say in a stentorian voice, "Let me tell you about the infinity of God," as if I were talking about someone who is 'up there,' 'out there,' elsewhere. If you have a sense of the ever-presentness of God, then you can *address* God.

Even now, as I am talking to you, I feel as if I'm looking up to God and God is saying: "Okay, Zalman. Carry on. This is good. Yes, they'll get it this way. They have the same the same equipment you have."

So you pray before you practice. How do you do that? By saying: "I make myself transparent to the divine light that wants to reach my heart. I open myself to that part of me that is already enlightened, existing at some point on the timeline that I haven't yet experienced, but which I know is there because, in eternity, what is in my future is already the present."

These are the kinds of inner workings that become the tools for greater awareness.

The Body

I want to come back to the issue of the body, because without the body, we can't do anything.

What's the afterlife like? The afterlife is seeing the movie of what you did in this lifetime. If you did good

8

and joyful things, you're in paradise. If you did not, you're in hell. There, we can't do anything new. Here is where we do it, and the body gives us the opportunity.

Take a look; it is not only my body that is here right now. It's also what I've eaten, and what the farmer did to grow that food, and what the cow ingested. You see, I'm a funnel from the environment to consciousness in my body, but everything has to go through the body. So I give it a lot of credit, and I want to make sure that I will be able to re-call my bodily experiences of spiritual things.

I'll give you an example.

If I begin to sing the evening melody of Rosh Hashanah, I am soon in touch with the High Holy Days. I begin to feel like I want to *shuckle* and *davven,* swaying back and forth in the prayer of that season. I want to because the melody has accessed the file in my body named "Evening Melody of Rosh Hashanah," and brings with it all the associated feelings and experiences of the High Holy Days.

So, when you go to a *shul,* when you're involved in a ritual, when you *davven* or meditate at home, try to locate the best memories of your experiences of these things in your body so that you can reconnect to them and add to their texture.

There is a prayer in the *siddur* which is said after we have relieved ourselves in the bathroom, washed our hands, and come out. In it, we say:

"We worship You, *Yah,* cosmic Majesty. You have created human beings with wisdom, and put into our bodies passages and ducts. All this is transparent to You. If but one of these would clog, or one of these would leak, we could not live; so we thank You for the miraculous order that You put into our body. *(With the in-breath and the out-breath, with pulse speed, and with neurons talking to*

9

each other, we say:) We worship You, the healer of all flesh, who does astonishing things."

If you can get a sense of that gratitude, you'll see why I want to get into the issue of where we are with our bodies.

Feelings in Meditation

Now, some of you who have heard a lot about meditation in our culture today might ask, "Do I always have to be calm and relaxed to get myself into the presence of the living God?" The answer is absolutely not.

Sometimes you're 'down and out,' feeling like the song says, "Nobody knows the troubles I've seen." And to whom should I go and talk about that? I suspect we would have a lot less depression in the world if people who feel downcast would be able to say, "Let me go and talk to God about it." When we have a sense that someone is really listening, then we can truly express what we feel: "I don't know which way to go; please, dear God, help me!"

The every-day God is also an important God. Most people think of God only as something special for the *shul* on *yontif,* to be saved for the synagogue on holidays. But the every-day God is even more important. There is a prayer in the *siddur* that says, "Your holy one's praise You everday." *Ukedoshim bkhol yom y'hal'lukha selah.* But this sentence can also be read, "Those who are holy praise you in the every-day." This is a very simple, 'blue jeans' holiness, and that's what God desires more than the big *yontif* productions.*

So you don't have to feel especially serene in order to do your practice. In fact, you can say, "I'm frustrated,

---

* We have this in Isaiah, chapter 1: *What need have I of your sacrifices? You're coming to celebrate and your hands are full of blood.* We have to live a good life and that's in the every-day situation.

God and I don't know who to tell about it; if I were to say it out loud, everyone would say I'm complaining, but I'm really am and I need to talk about it."

Can you see how doing this seriously, with your feelings fully engaged, can take you to a different place?

The other day someone was telling me, "I have real trouble with prayer."

"Good!" I said, "I'm glad that it gives you trouble. If it didn't, then it would be much worse. So come, let's go for a walk."

Here in Boulder there are such beautiful places to walk. Not too far from my home, there's a little lake where I do my daily walk. Sometimes the water is so calm that it is like a mirror, and I can see the Flatirons, the local peaks reflected in it. And sometimes the moon from night before is still hanging there while the sun is rising behind me in the east; it is so beautiful.

So I turn to my friend while we are looking at this lake and say, "Do you appreciate *this?*"

He said, "Yes, I appreciate it."

"Well, how about saying: 'God, I appreciate how you have made all of this beauty."

That's the beginning. When you're feeling good, when you are in euphoria, you can always say: "I appreciate this; I really appreciate this." When you begin with appreciation, the door opens up for more serious prayer.

Cells of the Greater Body

There is another element that I'd like to bring to your attention. Ever since the Renaissance, we have made the individual ego of paramount concern. In the Declaration of Independence, it says: "We hold these truths to be self-evident, that all men are created equal, that they are endowed by their Creator with certain unalienable Rights, that among these are Life, Liberty and the pursuit of

11

Happiness." Well this is good; it's much better than allowing some people to enslave others. Nevertheless, we should not see ourselves at the top of the scale because we are so endowed by the Creator; we have to remember the Creator.

Even before we get to God, we have to remember that there is another a sublime consciousness, much greater than ours. All of us are cells of a larger body, the body of our mother the Earth, who is now ailing. She is sick and she needs our help. Once we realize that we are not the ones who 'call the shots,' but that we collaborate in an organismic way with everything in this system, then our situation becomes much more balanced.

If we didn't have this environment, we would die from entropy. So we are in exchange with the whole chain of being on this planet, and we are integral to it. Those who see themselves as truly separate are not likely to be able to get into any kind of serious spirituality. When I think of the God I worship, I don't think of the infinite, cosmic, super-duper God; I think of the God who makes Earth renew herself, who is trying to wake us up in time to prevent global warming, and who brings us into a more intimate relationship with that body in which we live and that gives us life. When I think of *Ribbono shel Olam*, the master of the world, it is the God that keeps this world going. And the best way in which I can serve that God is through being integral.

This is why I'd like you to be good Jews. For once we understand the totality of life, then we realize that every religion is essential; every religion is a vital organ of the planet. The people who used to promote triumphalism in Judaism claimed that *Mashiah*, the Messiah will come one day all the Gentiles will find-out how wrong they are! And others did it as well. The Christians spoke of Jesus' 'Second Coming,' and Muslims spoke of the *Mahdi* in the same way. But now we must learn to think of all religions as integral to the planet.

12

Suppose I am a cell in a vital organ of the body; let's say the liver. If the liver is healthy, then the lungs are healthier, and the kidneys are healthier, and the heart is healthier, and the brain is healthier. Each organ is integral to the greater life-process. Likewise, we as individuals are integral to the life of the planet.

Once we get into this place, then we ask the question: "So why do we have to be Jewish?" The answer is, "Because we are a part of the vital organ organ called 'Judaism,' and we must be good Jews and keep the organ healthy, just as Muslims must be good Muslims, keeing that organ healthy. Sadly, there is a major sickness in Islam today, and the forces of integration are struggling with the separatist, 'rogue cells.' But all of us have an inflammation in the form of fundamentalism today. They want to take us back to an earlier view of life on the planet, when we said, "*We* are special, and we have the right to be on top," instead of saying, "We are integral."

All of this is just an introduction. In my next talk, I am going to discuss the vocabulary of Davvenology. Today, you don't have to translate words like *yoga, karma,* or *dharma;* they've simply become a part of common parlance. But so much of the language of Judaism's inner life has not, so this is what I'm going to deal with next.

In the meantime, if you would think of that for which you need a blessing at this moment, and if you would bring that into your heart, making it a vessel to receive the blessing, then I would like to be the instrument of blessing. It is not that I am offering my own blessing, but that I am doing what the Torah says: "And the LORD spoke to Moses, saying: Speak to Aaron and his children: Thus shall you bless the children of Israel, and say to them: may the LORD bless you and keep you; may the

LORD turn His face on you and favor you; may He lift you up into His presence and grant you peace. *Amen.*"*

Whatever blessing you need, may it come down to you. As the Torah says, "Put My name on the children of Israel and I shall bless them," says God.

Many *b'rokhes* to you—*shalom, shalom.*

Question and Answer Session

Question: You said that one of the ways to open prayer, to deepen it, is to have appreciation. I find myself at a place in my life where I don't have much appreciation. I see a beautiful landscape and I just think of all my pain and sorrow, in that self-centered way. So how would you deal with that?

Reb Zalman: Well, this has to do with steering the mind. It's like you have an itch. The itch is "I'm not happy." So obviously, when you are scratching that itch, you can't go to the place of happiness.

Now let me show you something.

Someone steps on your toe and then takes their foot off of it. *Ah-h-h,* it feels so good when they remove their weight from it. In reality, the body is usually feeling good. The reason we are not aware of it is because our reticular formation system, in the cerebellum, is tuning-out our steady-state of good feeling. So if it's a steady-state, we are rarely aware of it. But if you steer your mind and say, "What's good around me? Where doesn't it hurt? Where is it truly beautiful?" and offer a heartfelt thank you, that's already a beginning.

In some cases it is also good to remember that there are others worse off. This is not to belittle our own pain,

* Numbers 6:22-27.

but to bring a little perspective to it. After all, most of us are so much better off than many people in Biafra today, in south-eastern Nigeria. Clearly, there are some people in the world today who would wish to have our *tzores*, our troubles.

So often, the mind is just not agile enough; it always wants to stay in the place of the smaller, childish ego. But once you get away from that, and you start putting things into a larger perspective, into an organismic view of the whole world, then it's not so bad. And if you're not feeling good, it is a sign that the world and the body are telling you to do something about it.

Question: I'm very curious about the mirror neurons you were speaking about, and how we can meet in a 'non-local' space. Who is that 'we' that is meeting? In that world-view that this is a meeting-ground, and it's done with mirrors, what is that self? What is that being, or that awareness?

Reb Zalman: You know, there are some people who talk a lot about Emptiness and the non-egoic states. But when someone tells me there is no ego, and then I step on their toe, all of a sudden they have an ego!

What Daniel Goleman* is telling us about the mirror neurons has to do with neurology, that this happens in the brain. When I was saying that they are non-local phenomena—if I would have said this in 1930, people would've said, "You're crazy. You're nuts." But in today's post-quantum era, I don't have to be ashamed to say that. Larry Dossey** was in Boulder recently and gave a wonderful talk about intimations of the future, and how is it that some people are able to get those dreams and premonitions. Basically, it is because our soul is

---

* Psychologist and author of *Emotional Intelligence*.

** A medical doctor known for his books on non-local healing. He is the author of *Healing Words* and *The Power of Premonitions*.

wider than our present circumstances. For instance, the Zalman-field extends far beyond the confines of my body.

Now if I try to illustrate non-local phenomena, talking about the morphogenic field and the 'hundredth-monkey,' then it's really clear. And if I were to ask what it is that we need at this time in the political and social arenas, which seem burdened by negativity right now. With regard to radical Islam and the Middle East, people keep asking: "How do we defend ourselves? Can we send more soldiers into Afghanistan?" If we keep on thinking this way, we're only putting more of that out into the world. What we need to do is 'change the diapers' of our minds. That is to say, when the mind gets filled-up with *you know what*, then the only thing to do is 'change the diapers.'

I remember the Maharishi Mahesh Yogi* once asked a thousand of his people to meditate on peace during a difficult period between Israel and Palestine and it made a difference. He pointed out that if only 1% of humanity were to meditate, everything would change. People don't really believe that there is more than the physical realm, but if they were to be able to own that there is more, then perhaps we might create a social, critical mass of thinking, allowing us to make all the changes that we need to make. At least, I believe that.

Question: I'm thinking back to what you said about the sanctuary for God being a place of vulnerability, a space inside that's like a sore wound. Chogyam Trungpa** talked about a soft spot, or this raw, open wound. There's also the idea of going further back from the face we show the world. I'm aware that I feel in my day-to-day life a

---

* A Hindu *guru*, primarily known as the founder of Transcendental Meditation (TM), and for his association with the Beatles.

** The Tibetan Buddhist master who founded Naropa University and authored the influential book *Cutting Through Spiritual Materialism*.

huge, huge stigma to show the outer face and to have basically bundles and bundles of insulation around the vulnerability. I wondered if you could say something in relation to how to be in the world and cultivate that space.

Reb Zalman: Survival in the world right now is difficult. This society is not exactly the kind of society in which we can dare to be in a vulnerable place. By right, it should be that when we come to a spiritual group with whom we are in a loving relationship, we should be able to be vulnerable and open to feeling. But when I reflect on the way in which people go to synagogue or churches, I see that they are very defended. They sit very tight. They are so aware that everyone else is looking at them that they stay very stiff and don't open themselves up. Then they ask: "Why is it that I go to synagogue and I just 'spin my wheels'? Nothing much is happening for me." They are being driven by the survival based, 'reptilian system' within us, and have not even entered into this celebrative 'limbic system.'

For that kind of vulnerability, you need a good friend. It is so wonderful when you have a friend to whom you can say, as a child might, "Hey, look at my boo-boo." Likewise, the adult needs to be able to show a friend where it hurts, to own that, and not simply push it down. For, as I own it and show it to someone else, I feel the empathy of the other person, and my burden gets lighter. And then the two friends might pray that this burden be lightened, bringing both of their prayers together at that time. It doesn't have to be very fancy; it might be as simple as: "Dear God, Yankele is hurting. Please lift the burden from him, or give him the strength to carry it, whatever is necessary for his highest good, and the highest good of all the people he's in touch with." More words are not necessary, as long as I do this with the immediate sense that God really cares and is here, now. Many people don't have that sense of immediacy. You really have to work a little in order to get to that feeling. As I was saying in the beginning, "This is being monitored for quality purposes," i.e., if I see myself in the presence of God, then I can't be lost.

When my Rebbe* was imprisoned by the secret police in Soviet Russia, a policeman was threatening him with a gun, and he said to him: "I'm not afraid of you. You see, if I had many gods to serve and only one world to serve them in, I would be afraid. But I have but one God to serve and many worlds to serve Him in, so I'm not afraid." Do you get the idea? He couldn't have said it if he had felt that God wasn't there for him at that moment. That is what we can learn when we talk about *shiviti*.

Later, we'll go much deeper into how to place ourselves in the presence of God.

---

* Rabbi Yosef Yitzhak Schneersohn of Lubavitch (1880-1950), the 6th Lubavitcher Rebbe.

Second Talk
The Vocabulary of Davvenology

*"Concerning You, my heart has said: It is Your presence that I seek; do not forsake me, don't leave me behind. You have been my help, you have rescued me, God of my salvation."**

This has to do with *davvenen*; but what does the word *davvenen* mean? Well, if you go into a *Heymishe shul*, a warm and friendly synagogue of the traditional type, and ask what the people doing there, they will say that they are *davvenen*. The word covers so many things: it is both deeply engaged prayer and worship, and also just what you do when you put on a *tallit* and sway back and forth, raising your voice in prayer.

Though the origins of the word are unclear, I believe it comes from the Latin, *divinum*, 'to do the divine thing.' This is true of a number of words in the Jewish lexicon. For instance, after you have eaten, you *bentsh*, or say the grace after the meal. This is derived from the Latin, *benedictio*, to say the 'benediction,' the 'good word.'

When *I* speak about *davvenen*, I am talking about an inner process that goes way beyond ordinary prayer and worship; it is something that encompasses one's entire spiritual life. My sense is that a person can recognize that one who is *davvenen* is actually in touch with God. Even when they are walking in the street, they are nevertheless connected to God, and are *davvenen*; it is a constant element in their lives.

---

* Psalms 27:7-9.

19

Now, when we talk about *davvenen,* one of the things it brings to mind is what we want to achieve in it. If you ask people who are good in *davvenen,* they will tell you, "I want to be in *d'veikut* with God; I want to have *d'veikut.*"

D'veikut

The root of the word *d'veikut* is D-B-Q, which connects it to a whole family of Hebrew words that give us the sense that it has something to do with 'sticking,' 'glue,' 'adhering,' 'being close to,' 'being connected in a cozy way.'

When I shift one letter of the root, and make it H-B-Q, we get Hebrew words that mean, 'hug' or 'embrace.' And if we make it A-B-Q, we get 'wrestling,' as in the biblical moment when our father Jacob *vayeA-B-Q* with the angel.

But when we are talking about *d'veikut* in *davvenen,* the idea is that of 'sticking,' 'adhering' to God, a devotional 'clinging.' It has a sense of "What can I bring to You, God? I love you so much; I want to give you all that I can." *Mah ashiv la'Ha'Shem*? What can I give you?

The word also has a social meaning. If I want to be deeply connected to my teacher, my Rebbe, I might ask, "How can I be in *d'veikut* with my teacher?" That is to say, I am trying to imitate and emulate my teacher.* Of course, this is not a 'cheap imitation,' something *Ersatz.* This is imitation in the sense in which Thomas à Kempis used it in his classic work, *The Imitation Of Christ,* of *following, emulating, tuning-in.*

When I make a telephone call, I am creating a *d'veikut* between myself and the other person on the line. Through the telephone line, we connect. In the same way, when I want to learn from my teacher, the best way for me to learn is to open my capacity for receiving.

---

* In Tibetan Buddhism, this is often called Guru Yoga.

There is a wonderful story about professor Gershom Scholem, the great academic scholar of Kabbalah.* When he first came to Israel, he wanted to study with a kabbalist. So he asked one of the teachers of Kabbalah in Jerusalem, "In which way would you want to teach me?" And the kabbalist answered, "The only way in which I will teach you is if, for the next two years, you won't ask me any questions."

You see, if Scholem were asking questions in order to fit what he was learning into his own system, the one that he brought with him from academia, he would never learn what the kabbalist was trying to teach him. He would simply hold on to the previous matrix of the learning. So, it isn't only the content, but the attitude, the approach to the text, the attunement to the holiness inherent in it. That is a most important thing, for *d'veikut* is like emulating the other.

Sometimes the Rabbis of the Talmud ask, "How can one be close to God if God is infinite?" So they answer, "Find one of the divine modes and emulate that mode." *Mah hu rahum af attah rahum, mah hu hannun af attah hannun.* "As God is kind and gracious, so you become kind and gracious; as He is compassionate and merciful, so you become compassionate and merciful."** In this way, I stretch myself to fit the divine template.

Consider this: if I were to grow up without any input from outside, I would grow up pretty wild, because all that I would have are my own impulses. But when I see a great person and I say to myself, "When I grow up, I want to be just like him," then I am stretching myself into that template.

I once had a friend who was pretty obese. He was a nice guy and we had wonderful conversations, but I had

* Gershom Scholem (1897-1982). Sometimes I speak of him as a 'Kabbal-ologist,' because of his wonderful bibliographical and historical work with kabbalistic texts.

** Talmud, Shabbat 13b.

not seen him for a while. One day, I was invited to do a wedding, and while I was there, a man comes over to me in a very friendly way, like I have known him forever, but I don't recognize him. Nevertheless, I pretend that I do, and we have a nice, gentle conversation. Later, he called me on the telephone and he said, "I realized that you didn't recognize me." Now it all started to make some sense, and I asked him, "How did you become so handsome and thin?" And he said, "I asked God how would He like to see me, and I fastened on to that image."

Do you get that? *Hadbek b'middotav.* I measure myself in God's view and decide to shape myself according to that template. So this is a part of *d'veikut.*

Kavvanah

When you talk to someone about a good davvener, they will often say, "He davvens with *kavvanah.*" Now, the word *kavvanah* can have many meanings. It can mean 'fervor,' as in "He davvens with fervor, putting all his heart and emotion in to it." But it's most precise meaning has to do with 'intention.' When someone is using a bow and arrow, and is aiming at a target, they are *m'khavven.* *L'khavven* means 'to aim.' What is your *aim* in what you are doing? What have you got in mind?

Kavvanah also has a sense of fulfilling a *mitzvah* without extrinsic motives or ideas. It is not done for the sake of having others see me do it, or so that I should acquire a good reputation. I have put my *kavvanah,* my intention into the act of the *mitzvah.*

It also has the sense of not being distracted by externals: "That is the direction I want to go in, and I'll go there, no matter what wants to distract me or turn me aside." So to say that I will *davven,* or meditate, or study with *kavvanah,* all have to do with a total involvement in that activity.

Most people are freewheeling, as far as the mind is concerned; they don't hold on to the steering wheel. Wherever their mind wants to go, they let it go. But if you want to do the inner work, you have to learn how to steer your mind, how to really guide your mind. And in order to do that, people have to learn to direct it in shorter moments. For instance, "Can I keep my *kavvanah* on the words *Shma Yisrael, Adonai Eloheynu, Adonai Ehad*? Paying attention to the word *ehad* (one) for a half a minute, thinking about the oneness, the uniqueness, the totality, the All, without going away from that?" This is how *kavvanah* gets extended over time. If you want to learn how to steer your consciousness over longer periods, this will help you in your *d'veikut*, and in your *hitbonenut*.

Hitbonenut

The root of the word *hitbonenut* comes from the biblical usage *hitbonanta al m'qomo v'eynenu*, "I will focus my looking on his place and won't find him." You get the sense that it is a kind of meditation that isn't *thinking* as much as *contemplation*—I want to *see* it.

This is the real difference between the study of Talmud and the study of Zohar. When you learn Talmud, it says *Ta sh'ma'*, "Come and *listen!*" That is to say, I'll explain something to you. But in the Zohar it says, *Ta haziy*, "Come and see!" Contemplation is seeing with the inner eye; it is to look intensely at something.

Suppose I want to talk to you about how the infinite becomes involved with the finite. This is pretty abstract material. Or, say I want to talk about the *sefirot*, the Four Worlds and their interaction; there is an idea-cluster, I may have lots of wonderful ideas, but how do all they all fit together in the big picture? It is not enough to have the information in my head; there has to be a way in which I can *behold* the ideas.

To *be-hold* them means that I can hold their form before my mind's eye—*Shiviti Ha'Shem l'negdi tamid*, "I

23

have *be-held Ha'Shem* before me always." *Be-holding* is happening when the ideas I've gotten from my study of various holy books, or heard from great teachers, arouse insights of my own. For there are times when my intuition opens me up to something beyond, and it flashes in my awareness. If I don't pay attention to that flashing idea-cluster, it will quickly disappear. I must take hold of it immediately and *be-hold* it for a while, so that I can install it in my memory, fastening it in *hitbonenut* (contemplation).

When I behold these contemplations with intensity, then the idea becomes a reality for me. This is important: I can study everything in the world, and it is nothing more than ideas; but when I study Torah, I want to be in *relationship* with God. I should almost *see* that idea-cluster before me; it should be a reality for me.

I'll give you such an example.

Adon Olam Asher Malakh b'terem kol y'tzir nivra: "Lord of the world, You reigned before there was any creation." *L'yet na'assah b'hftzo kol azai melekh shmo nikra*: "When by Your will everything was made, we called You our King (in the present)." *V'aharey kikhlot hakol l'vado yimlokh nora*: "When it is all over, in the end, You alone will rule for ever."*

Who was God before the Big Bang? That's *Adonai Malakh*. God's past is before the Big Bang. From the Big Bang to the last black hole is God's present. God's future is after the last black hole, when everything will be reabsorbed, and once again, God will be alone.

Now if you will try and contemplate this, you will get a sense of how vast the divine present really is. And if you can stay with that for a while, looking intensely at it, many things can happen. You may disappear in this thought, because all is God and God is all—*God is*. Or, you may not disappear in your contemplation. You

---

* *Adon Olam,* a hymn for the Jewish liturgy.

24

might say, "I am here and I am needed to do something for God's sake, and I dedicate myself completely to that." Or, I might address God in the present, and say, *Barukh attah,* "I praise You." Or, I can also look at all of Creation and the cosmic radiation resulting from the Big Bang, filtering-in to us from outer space.

These are great contemplations, and when they become so real to me that I actually feel that they are really true, they become the reality with which I live, and this *hitbonenut* makes an impact on my feelings; my heart has participated in that *hitbonenut.*

I'll give you two examples of this kind of impact.

Imagine, a friend of mine asks me, "Did you hear about the big lottery?" "No," I say, not very interested. But then he asks, "Do you remember how I was gonna buy you a ticket?" A little more interested, I listen up. "Well, your tickect won!" he says. Immediately I am flooded with excitement. It is no longer a *mere idea.*

Or, imagine you have a friend who is a pathologist, and you come and visit him at work one day. He says, "Come, let me show you something." He takes you to a microscope and shows a slide. Then he says, "See, this is where the healthy tissue is, and this is the cancerous tissue." And you say, "That's very interesting." Then he says, "This is the slide from your biopsy." All of a sudden, the *merely interesting* becomes *totally absorbing,* having implications for your whole life.

This is the kind of impact that is desired in *hitbonenut.* So if I come to the end of my *davvenen* and I don't feel that the words have taken me to an encounter that reality, then the *davvenen* was just so many words.

Hitbodedut

Hitbodedut is making a place in which I can disconnect from my social connections and other sensations. All I want to do in that place is contemplate. Today, it is the

25

Bratzlaver Hasidim who use this word the most, but it actually has a long and venerable history, going back to the time of Elijah and Elisha, and even further back to the time of Samuel the prophet.

He used to lead a group of people called the *b'nai ha-n'vi'im*, the 'sons of the prophets,' who wanted to learn about the inner worlds. Later on, we find that the authors of the Dead Sea Scrolls were doing similar things: sitting in silence and solitude, and doing their contemplation. At that time, people would go into the desert and sit in a cave in order not to be distracted by externals. From there it was the flight of the *one* to the *One*.

If you were to ask the hermit, "What are you doing?" He would say, "I am dwelling here in solitude." If you asked him, "How can you bear to be alone?" He would respond: "How could I be alone? God is with me; I am *not* alone." That element of being in such a connection with God was called *hitbodedut*.

Nowadays, most praying is done with prayer books. What's the problem with that? It is a problem if a person thinks that reciting *Ashrey* from the *siddur* is what constitutes a relationship with God. What if we never had a prayer book? All we need to be aware of is that we know that we are getting the attention of God, and God will listen to what we have to say.

Oy! How I would go to the essentials at this point! I would say, "Dear God, I need Your energy and Your strength and Your wisdom." And I would begin to talk in this direct way, pouring out my heart to God. Often, I switch to Yiddish. My Yiddish just expresses my heart-feeling for God better than my English. And when I am talking to God in this way, the tears begin to flow because I am so involved in the words I am offering before the living God, and am certain that I am not just talking to the wall!

Reb Nahman of Bratzlav would encourage his disciples to go out into the woods at night when no one could hear them and pray in this way. When the Ba'al Shem Tov was a child, he would skip *heder* from time to time and go to the forest. And once, he found a man talking to God in the forest alone. This made a great impression on him, and he too would talk to God in nature. Sometimes this kind of prayer is stronger than anything you will say out of the prayer book.

T'fillah

Now we come to the word 'prayer,' *t'fillah. T'fillah* could be the text of a prayer; it could be the function of prayer. Some people derive the word from *p'lilim*, meaning 'judges.' That is to say, prayer has to do with 'self-judgment' and renewal in the presence of God. Other people say it has something to do with making something stick together, as in *ha-tofel kli heres*, to log-on to God, as it were.

Siddur

Keeping that definition of prayer in mind, I want to talk about the prayers prescribed by the Rabbis, which are found in the Jewish prayer book, called a *siddur*. *Siddur* comes from the word *seder*, which means 'order.'

In the past, *siddurim* varied according to ethnic communities. The Jews from Poland had one *siddur*, and the Jews of Germany had another. The differences were only small changes in words and the order of the prayers. These were called a difference in *rite*. Therefore, there was a Polish rite, a German rite, and a Yemenite rite. Nowadays, many individual communities and commitment-groups have their own *siddurim*, some of them desiring to have more inclusive, egalitarian language, for instance. It is very important for them to be able to mention, not only the male ancestors, but also the female ancestors in their prayer.

No matter which *siddur* you use—whether Renewal, Reconstructionist, or Reform—all will have the same basic scaffolding, even though some of the texts will differ.

Right now, I am looking at the morning prayers, which are in the kabbalistic *world of action,* and begin with the use of the body. Then they move on to the *world of feeling* and appreciation as we say the psalms. Then one goes to the *world of mind* and contemplation before coming to the *Amidah,* where we are 'standing' before the living God in the *world of being,* where you can, like a child, ask for what you really need. When you look at the *Amidah,* you will see how so much asking is really spelled-out there—almost everything that we need.

If you give yourself permission to 'lift-off' from the words of the *siddur,* it is better, because then you can let loose according to the inspiration you receive as grace at that moment. And you can always go back to the *siddur* if you lose the inspiration. But if you just go with the depth of the words, "The soul of every living being praises You," and "You are God from one world to the other," you have got more than enough to contemplate.

The *siddur* for the High Holidays and the pilgrimage holidays is called a *mahzor,* and contains different prayers and specific adaptations for these holidays.

Most of the time people chant the words of the *siddur.* Why? Because, the words by themselves are too dry. If I were to take the lyrics of a love song and simply *say* them to my wife, they would sound funny. But if I were to sing them, I could put something behind the words; I could sing them with feeling. Therefore, when you come to *davven,* and you want to say, for instance, *Yishtabah Shimkhah la'ad malkeynu,* "Your name be praised, majestic one," then the melody that you are going to use needs to be harmonious with the words.

It is really worthwhile for you to take some of the holy poetry that is in the *siddur* and to put it to different melodies. This will help you to appreciate the rhythm and feeling of the words.

Niggun

Professor Abraham Joshua Heschel used to say that a *niggun* is "a tune flowing in search of its own unattainable end,"* because when you come to the end of a *niggun* you start it all over again. Like my friend Reb Shlomo Carlebach would say, "A *niggun* is never finished."** Once it ends, you want to go back and sing it over and over again.

There are several kinds of *niggunim,* depending on the circumstances in which they are to be sung. Most often you find *niggunim* around the festive table, where they are spoken of as *z'mirot.* There are wonderful poems that people have matched to melodies. We sing them in different kinds of melodies which betray different ethnic influences. This one has a Russian flavor; another has a Hungarian flavor. We do these things around the table because a dinner table is considered an altar, and around the altar the Levites used to sing during the offering of the sacrifices. If a meal is served on *Shabbat* or *yontif,* you will always find people singing table hymns, which we call *tish niggunim,* or 'table melodies.'

Now imagine that *Shabbat* is ending and we no longer have any artificial light in our little *shtib'l.* The only light is coming from the *Ner Tamid* on top of the Holy Ark. We are sitting around the table at *Shalosh S'udot,* the third meal. The food is not what is important at this meal; it is the mood, which says, "*Oy! Shabbat* will soon be over!" From where will we take the holy energy that we need

---

* In his classic book, *The Earth is the Lord's: The Inner World of a Jew in Eastern Europe.*

** Shlomo Carlebach (1925-1994), peace be upon him, composed over 300 *niggunim,* most of which are now in the public domain because no one knows who created them. Nevertheless, they are sung everywhere because they bring you into your feelings. And that is the point of a *niggun.*

during the week? From these beautiful melodies, full of longing. So much yearning comes out in them. You simply sing these melodies together and there is no need for talking. Then there wells up in people the sense of longing which can tune one's spirituality for the whole week.

My criticism of a lot of modern spirituality is that there is no longing in the method. So many teachers of spirituality work with self-satisfied people who are saying: "Now *I am* going to meditate." It is often missing the ingredient that asks, "How will I become what I need to become? How will I serve in the way in which I need to serve?" The *niggunim* that 'ask' these questions are what you call *ga'agu'im*, 'longing' *niggunim*, and they are very beautiful. They create the shared sacred model for us by raising up an unspoken prayer.

When people think that we are merely singing melodies, they are wrong. If I am singing the Tzemah Tzedek's* *D'veikut Niggun,* words even cannot approach what I am saying about how "I long to be how You would want me to be God" without words in the *niggun.* These are the unspoken prayers of contemplative *niggunim.*

There are also some *niggunim* that are based on traditional modes. For instance, if I begin to sing a High Holiday tune for the evening prayer, in my imagination I hear it as if it were played by an orchestra. I can hear the brass and the fanfare as if proclaiming a welcome to the Divine King into our midst. This is what we do on Rosh Hashanah night. But we are not the first to sing this melody. If I look into the genetic line of that melody, it would take me to my father and my grandfather, my great-grandfather and well beyond; for all of my Ashkenazic ancestors used this melody on Rosh Hashanah night.

---

* Rabbi Menachem Mendel Schneersohn I of Lubavitch (1789-1866), the third Lubavitcher Rebbe.

This repetition through the generations has created what Rupert Sheldrake calls a morphogenetic field. When I enter into that field, I move from 'commodity time' to 'sacred time.' I move into the vibration of Rosh Hashanah when I sing this melody with *Kavvanah* and energy. Therefore, these modes are powerful stimulants. We call them *nussah*. They are clues to the worshiper on how to fine-tune his or her inner being.

Imagine it is a *Shabbat* before the new moon, and you are saying that prayer for the new moon, the prayer which begins with the words, "May it be thy will Lord our God to renew for us the coming month and grant us life and health." The Cantor begins the prayer with a pleading recital. The worshipers want to be included in what the Cantor is praying for, so they afford the Cantor a harmonious chord in a minor key, and the Cantor weaves this pleading prayer around their sound. From time to time you might even hear a sob to punctuate the pleading.

The *nussah* melodies are ways to entrain us in specific ways of being.

B'rakhot

What are *b'rakhot*? Or, in the more colloquial Yiddish, *b'rokhes*? The word is derived from the Hebrew *berekh*, which means 'knee.' So when we say, *Barukh attah Ha'Shem*, we could translate it literally as, 'kneeled-to are You,' or 'Worshipped are You.'

There is also another meaning for *b'rakhot* derived from the word *brekhah*, 'a pool,' or 'a channel of water flowing down.' What this means is that I want to bring down grace from heaven, opening a channel for someone. That is to say, God has good things 'in store' for you, and those good things belong to you. Thus, when we give people *b'rakhot*, we facilitate the bringing down of what is already waiting in heaven for the person.

31

This is what we call *bentshen*, the term used for the grace after meals. This comes from benediction, 'saying good words.' What it really means is that there is such goodness in store for you from God, but all of it doesn't always come down. Sometimes there is something blocking it. So to create a channel for it, I speak the *b'rakhah*, that *bentshen*. It is not *my* gift to you, but rather *God's* gift that I help to bring down. Thus, we may say along with the Torah, "Speak to Aaron and to his sons, and say unto them, 'Thus shall you *bentsh* the children of Israel saying to them, 'May the Lord *bentsh* you and protect you.' " After which it says, "You will put My Name on the children of Israel and I Myself will do the blessing."* You see, the blessing does not come from the *kohen*, from the priest; it comes from God.

Now how do we use the blessings that the tradition has handed down to us? When we say, *Barukh Attah*, "Blessed are You" and mention God's name, the emphasis is on *Attah*, 'You.' That is to say, I place myself in Your Presence. And before I eat an apple, I say, *Barukh Attah Ha'Shem elokeinu melekh ha'olam Borei p'ri ha'etz*. Here I value the word *borei*, not in the past, but in the present. Thus, "You, the Creator, are still 'creating' the apple that I am about to eat." So with every *b'rakhah* I am make, I put myself in a position to recognize that we are receiving a gift from our Creator.

When we are performing a *mitzvah*, like putting on the *t'fillin*, what are we saying a *b'rakhah* for? We want to thank God for commending us to wear *t'fillin*; we want to be able to say, "Dear God, by doing this act, I intend to fulfill Your sacred will; I want Your sacred will to enter into my arm and my head through the *t'fillin*."

Imagine I ask you to raise your arm. As you do so, you make it possible for my will to activate your hand. So it is when we do a *mitzvah*; our intention makes it possible for the divine will to enter our body and to do that

---

* Numbers 6:24-26.

mitzvah. This is how Rabbi Kalonymus Kalmish Shapira, the Piasetzno Rebbe, *alav ha'shalom,* explains how God is fulfilling all the *mitzvot.*[*] What it amounts to is that I want to be in touch with the divine will, to allow it to inhabit me, to be imminent and indwelling within me.

So when I need to make a *b'rakhah,* I say *Attah,* "You have sanctified us with Your commandments, and sanctified us in the same manner as a bridegroom who gives a ring to his bride." And God says, *Harey at m'kuddeshet li,* "You are wedded to me, and sanctified through this *mitzvah.*"

By making a *b'rakhah* before I partake of food, or when I am about to interact with a material object, I am admitting that I don't own it, that it isn't mine. Instead, I recognize God as the owner; and by saying the *b'rakhah,* I am receiving permission to use it. Moreover, by saying the *b'rakhah* before doing a *mitzvah,* I am becoming wedded to the Divine Will.

The other meaning for *b'rakhah* is seen on *Shabbat* when parents give a blessing to their children. We have all these *b'rakhot*-models taken from the Torah: Isaac giving a blessing to Jacob before his death, Jacob blessing his own children before death, and likewise with Moses.

Shul

Where do we meet for prayer? In the *shul.* I like the word *shul* better than temple or synagogue. *Shul,* 'school' implies that we are always learning. What do you get in a *shul?* You get the *siddur,* the prayer book, which is an *aid de memoir,* a way to keep you on track so that you might not lose your place while ascending the sacred ladder.

---

[*] Rabbi Kalonymus Kalmish Shapira of Piasetzno (1889-1944) was a *rebbe* during the Holocaust who authored the book, *Esh Kodesh.*

Minyan

Now when you are praying in a *shul*, you want to have a *minyan*, a prayer quorum. The Jewish desire to pray in a communal way is based upon a belief that says, when 10 people are gathered together in a *minyan*, they form one field, which allows the holy *Shekhinah*, the Divine Presence, to manifest.

Traditionally, a *minyan* consists of 10 men; but in Jewish Renewal (and other egalitarian *minyanim*) we count 10 human beings, ten committed Jews.

As I said, it is believed that there is a greater manifestation of the Divine Presence when 10 or more people are gathered together for prayer. But I want to suggest still another meaning for why we wish to *davven* with a *minyan*. Sometimes I am not fully present. But the likelihood is that someone else is fully present even when I am not. Thus, the *minyan* supports me in my *davvenen* even if I space-out in the middle.

Later, we will talk about Kabbalah and the *sefirot*, and about creating sacred space with candles, incense, and meditation.

Many *b'rokhes* to you — *shalom, shalom*.

Question and Answer Session

Question: You talked about *hitbodedut* and the *minyan* — that it is important to have both solitary prayer and communal prayer — How do you bridge the two?

Reb Zalman: Imagine I am a violinist who is about to give a concert. If I want to be good in the concert, I have to practice. If I don't practice alone, it is difficult to refine my style. But if I only practice alone, I do not learn from and become attuned to the orchestra. There is something that happens in solitude that I bring into the *minyan,* and there is something in the *minyan* that helps me in my solitude.

I had a friend, God bless his soul, he was a Sefardi who came from Holland and he was in a city where there was no daily *minyan,* and sometimes not even a *minyan* on *Shabbat.* He was a person who really loved God and wanted to pray. So I asked him, "What do you do?" He says, "I see myself in the great synagogue in Amsterdam and I pray there with all the people." In this case he was taking his own public prayer into the private realm.

Third Talk
What is Jewish Meditation?

In my previous talk, I briefly discussed *hitbonenut* meditation and spoke of how the *niggun* is supposed to create an affective atmosphere into which you can enter when you are contemplating something.

If I were to give you a dictionary definition of meditation, we would never get to the depth of what meditation is really about. But if I were to sing you a *niggun*, from openhearted place, we would begin to see very quickly what Jewish biblical meditation is really about.

At this point, many people have written about Jewish meditation; but I am still somewhat dissatisfied with what most of them have said, because it is often only Buddhist or Hindu meditation in Jewish clothing. For instance, instead of reciting *Om*, a *mantra* in Sanskrit, they might use *shal-Om*. This is fine, but there is so much more to Jewish Meditation.

First of all, the word 'meditation' did not have to be imported from the East; it was already in Psalm 19:15: "May the words of my mouth and the *meditation* of my heart be acceptable in Your sight O LORD." Notice that it says, "In Your sight O LORD." This is a very important phrase, for I invite God to witness my meditation.

We have had meditation all along. The intent of it was to become aware of those sentences in Torah that point to consciousness, specifically those that tell us to "remember." The Torah loves to use the word 'remember': "*remember* how you stood at Mt. Sinai," "*remember* how you went out of *Mitzrayim*," "*remember* the *Shabbat* to keep it holy!" Torah wants us to re-member, to re-

37

connect with these things and become one with them. So remembering is one of the most important features of Jewish meditation.

In computers, there is such a thing that as a 'memory resident program.' For instance, my computer has a virus detector, and it is a memory resident program. As soon as it becomes aware of a virus, an unwanted intruder, it tells me that I should quarantine that file because it will make trouble for the computer. The rest of the time, it is dormant, simply living in the computer's memory.

Can you imagine what it would be like to have memory resident programs in us? If I wanted to do something wrong, my *averah* virus-detector would sound an alarm and signal me to stop.

The problem is that most of the time, our value-ideas are not resident in memory; they don't sound an alarm when they are most needed. There is a strange discrepancy between our *is* and our *ought*, between what I *ought to do* and what I *am actually doing*.

How can I bring more *ought* into my *is*? How can I make my value-ideas memory resident so that I might serve God better?

This is why the Torah speaks of remembering! How can I make the things that I should remember memory resident? Well, if it "remember how you were at Sinai," then you should actually spend some time thinking about what was it like at *Har Sinai*. What was it like when the curtain parted between mundane reality and suddenly we saw God and the whole cosmos clearly? All that came with the word *Anokhi*, 'I Am That.' Then, the aperture closed again and we yearned to go back to that moment of opening, when we were able to see with our ears and hear with our eyes! In this way, we can make that moment resident in our memory.

So much of Biblical meditation is found in the phrase uttered by Moses, *v'yada'ata ha'yom v'hashevota al le-*

vavekha, "Know it today" — be aware of it, fully encounter it today — "and make it settle in your heart." And what is that that I should "know today and put into my heart"? "That *Yud-Heh-Vav-Heh* is *Elohim*." * That Creation is only God in the shape of Creation.

How do I know that? Because *Attah har'eta lada'at*, "You have made Yourself visible to me." ** If people say there is no God, it is because they have not spent any time trying to make themselves visible to God. It is not that God is invisible; we have made ourselves opaque, and in this way, we become unseeing and invisible.

If I say, "Look at me, God!" wanting to be totally transparent, then God can see me through and through — without any opaqueness — everything that I am, was, and will be. "Whatever is open to You" — *galluy v'yadu'a* — "it is totally transparent to You."

If I can get into that place, then I have made a connection with the *Attah har'eta lad'at* — "You have made Your Self visible to our awareness that, *Y-H-V-H* is *Elohim*. If I understand that process — even if I didn't do anything more, if there were no other meditation than this — then, when I look around and see finite people and finite things, I can say, "Hey God! Hi there, hi there." I can see God in every person and every object.

The Sanctuary

There is something important about being vulnerable. Many people, when they come to a *shul*, or *l'havdil*, a church, do not want to come vulnerable. Instead, they come with a lot of armour and protection: *This is how I am coming in and this is how I will leave.* There is a fear of being changed or transformed by the experience, and they don't want to give-up or surrender their public persona

---

* Deuteronomy 4:39.

** Deuternomy 4:35.

and self-concept. This is what you call *mitzvot anashim melummadah*, a rote kind of bourgeois participation.

If I am going to the place of vulnerability, I need to be *recalibrated*. Every once and a while, my sense of right and wrong gets mixed-up, and I am not sure which way is the right way. Or sometimes I have an outdated sense of right and wrong that comes from generations past that cannot help me today. So where do I go to recalibrate my sense of right and wrong? *To the encounter with God today!*

What do I want? I want to live my life in such a way that I will fulfill the purpose for which I was created. If I can do that, then I have done everything that I need to do. But if I really need to be recalibrated, and I come with the attitude, *Don't mess with my current calibration,* then no *shul* is not going to help me, no 'spirituality' is going help me. I have to make myself open first.

In this very special place, in which meditation is best done, in sacred solitude, I can go into my 'lonely place,' a place reserved only for me. If anyone else were to enter that place, they would almost certainly step on my heart, and trample my most tender feelings.

But where does *Ha'Shem* want the Divine Presence, the *Shekhinah* to dwell? *Davka,* precisely in that solitary place! God wants the Divine Presence to take up residence in my lonely place, where I am most tender, most precious, vulnerable, and sensitive. And I want to be a 'host' for God in that place, and think of God as the "Lord of Hosts."*

What is Meditation?

Now, if our minds are going to take up residence in that place, then we need to learn to *steer* them with *kavvanot,* holy intentions.

---

* This is a poor translation of *Adonai Tz'va'ot,* but I like it here, because it allows me to be a *host* for God, for the *Shekhinah,* in my heart.

In my first talk, I described an exercise that allows one to enter that place in the heart. For meditation is not so much in the brain as it is in the heart. We say, *hegyon libi le'fanekha*, "the meditation of my heart before You," because the heart has a lot more energy than the brain. When you take an electroencephalogram, you need much more power than you need when you take a cardiogram, because the heart pumps with a lot more energy. The truth of the matter is that, if I want something to be *real* in my life, it has to be much more than an idea in my head. Knowing the law of gravity and going for a walk integrate the sense of gravity for me. I walk because I *be-live* in gravity. Gravity is a reality for me. What if living in the *presence of the living God* was as real as gravity to me?

I once had a rolfer, Joseph Heller, a wonderful guy who started Hellerwork. He taught me that the basic law of the universe is love. So I said, "How do you get to that?" He said, "Because two bodies in space attract one another; this is the law of gravity." Just think of that sense of attraction.

We need to learn how to steer the mind and hold on to the intention, which is the work of the *kavvanah*. Once I wrote the following about meditation:

Perhaps a meditation is a daydream, a daydream of the Soul as the Beloved and G-d, the Lover — their meeting in the tryst of prayer, their yearning for one another after parting, a daydream of their being united again.

It is not so much that I am thinking good ideas, but I am having a daydream of how God loves me. What's so wonderful about daydreams is that they also get into the heart, and then they go into the body. I have a daydream about how we meet in a special place, about which, nobody else knows. And there, God and I meet in that tryst, in that loving place. And when our meeting has come to an end, for instance, when *Shabbat* is ending, there is a

41

sense of bittersweetness, followed by another daydream of being re-united.

What if children were encouraged to daydream in school? Let's say the teacher has just talked about the Alps, and all the animals there, and Johnny looks out the window with his finger in his mouth daydreaming. His teacher sees this and says, "Stop daydreaming." This is so silly, because he's just gone to the Alps and is seeing what he has learned in class! A good teacher would say to the class: "We've finished the unit. Now, take the next 10 minutes to daydream about what it is like to walk in the Alps." You see, that fills a need.

When people are in love with each other, they are always daydreaming: *When we meet again, what we will do together, and how we will do it?*

Or perhaps a meditation is the human soul becoming aware of its loneliness and anticipating its being united with the One Who transcends the all and conquers one's defences.

I think this is important, because most of us avoid the lonely place inside of us. It just hurts too much. But how are we going to do what we need to do in our meditation unless we go to that place? Nobody else knows what's going on in my mind, but I need to open my mind to God; I want so much to be known by God in this way. I become aware of my loneliness, and I have an anticipation of being united with the One who transcends it all and is able to come past my own defenses: *Dear God, do not let my resistance to You stop You from coming into my heart.*

Once a Christian nun told me that all of spiritual direction is really learning how to reduce one's resistance to God. Imagine if I were to say, "God, I'll do whatever you want me to do," and then a moment later, "But I hope You don't ask me to do that." We have our reservations, but we need to say, "I am prepared," even if we just sit with that for a while, allowing it to enter into our *kishkes*. This has a transformative power.

Or perhaps, again, it is a standing back with the whole of the cosmos before one's mind's eye as the heart is filled with the sheer joy of seeing the balance of the All and one's own self as part of it.

This is another form of meditation. If you take all the visions of the universe from Star Trek and Carl Sagan, seeing all those marvelous visions of the universe, and how everything is where it has to be, and you realize: *I, too, am part of this wondrous universe; and I am filled with joy at seeing this totality in which I participate; and I am grateful.*

Or perhaps it is a searching into one's own motives, values and wishes, with the light of the Torah against the background of the past.*

Another form of meditation is the inner work of checking-out one's motives, values and wishes: *Why am I doing this? What do I want?* If I check-out my own motives at this moment for talking about this subject, I realize this: I have been teaching people about *davvenen* for most of my life, and I want to leave something behind about this subject, because I know that I only have a limited amount of time. My horizon is getting smaller, and I want to make sure that the experience of my romance with God, my enchantment with holiness, will be passed on to others. So I do the checking-out work, and I see how this fits with Torah and our past.

Essentials of Meditation

Here are some of the *sine quibus non*, the essentials of meditation.

---

* All of these passages are drawn from the section, "What is Meditation?" in my book, *Gate to the Heart: An Evolving Process.*

43

All methods of introspection, of carving-out inner space are necessary and welcome. Unless I have inner space, I am not going to be able to meditate. Where do I go with my meditation? *Inner space.* Very few people have carved-out enough inner space for themselves. Sometimes it takes pain and *tzores* (trouble) to carve-out inner space, but I want to take that hiding-place inside my heart and make it larger, in order to accommodate more of the *Shekhinah,* to make it a sanctuary for the Divine Presence.

Every generic method that helps us carve-out more inner space is is good. I am not against sitting and observing the breath in silence, calming yourself and emptying your thoughts etc. But I do not believe that anyone can empty their thought-containers entirely today. We just get too much input from all the media around us. If I had to stand with a bucket and bail-out everything that that is coming in, it would be nearly impossible. What I *can* do is pay attention to particular kinds of things. Instead of *emptying* myself, I can *fill* myself with something, and that is easier.

I like to talk about how coffee can be 'vacuum packed' or 'pressure packed.' Coffee makers gave up on vacuum packing because it is much harder to produce a vacuum than to produce pressure with inert gas in the can. And when you open the can, the aroma is so powerful. Out comes that wonderful fragrance that we always look for in the cup, but never find outside of the can. There it is under pressure.

If I only have twenty minutes, and I want to use these for emptying, it is very difficult for most people. You don't often get past the business of life to the deeper areas. So I like to spend these twenty minutes focused specifically with *kavvanah.* This can make a big difference.

It is also necessary to steer the mind so I can do my homework on my behavior system, my morality system. The *examination of conscience* means that I have to go into places that make me anxious: *Why did I tell that half-truth? Why did I tell a lie? Why did I do this? Why did I do that?* I don't want to go there; it makes me anxious. But how am I going to change if I don't go into the anxious places? This is an important part of the inner work, and if you don't do this in the presence of God, then a lot of your spirituality will be like "whipped cream on garbage." The garbage is still rotting underneath.*

Jewish Meditation

What are the especially *Jewish* dimensions that we need to include in meditation? In the past, I have been a vocal critic of so-called 'Jewish meditation' that just seemed to be *Vipassana* (Buddhist-style meditation) with *shmaltz* on it. Doing Buddhist meditation in a *tallit,* in a prayer shawl doesn't make it Jewish. But doing it in the Presence of God at least adds a Jewish dimension to it.

Imagine I am doing *Vipassana* meditation, quieting the mind and watching the breath: *I calm myself, and I am paying attention to what arises.* Most of the time, people sit down on the cushion and close themselves off: *I don't want to know about anything else; I don't want to let anything in.* But that is not conducive to entering a state that is characterized by alpha or theta brain waves, because you're too tightly wound; nor is it the Buddhist ideal. It needs to breathe; it needs to be open.

Now, if you are Jewish, this openness is to God. And when thoughts and feelings arise in your meditation, you can release them to God: "God, here comes anger again . . . Here comes lust . . . Here comes boredom." It is not that I am simply acknowledging these things and releasing them into the ether, but I am releasing them to God. It is process that is open to a higher dimension, and I make a window for God to look into me as I'm meditating.

---

* A phrase coined by Bob Hoffman.

45

Now why should you want to bother with meditation in the first place? Because I think it is a *mitzvah*. It is a *mitzvah* to place oneself in the Presence of God. It is a *mitzvah* to work on moral transformation.

When you learn Rabbi Moshe Hayyim Luzzato's *Mesillat Yesharim*, the 'way of the upright,'* he points out that the most important thing is *shleymut ha'avodah*, the perfection of your service for God: What do I care what the outcome will be? I only care that I've been assigned to do this, and I want to do it right. I want to do a good day's work, as it were.

When a movie begins, the opening credits say, 'a production of . . .' And often it is three or four production companies who have joined together to produce a movie. I want to be able to say before the *davvenen*, "This is a production of *shleymut avodah*; it is meant to be in complete service to God." Then I can say, "And I want my *davvenen* to be according to the *nussah ha'Ari* today."** So you take care of all the credits beforehand, and that is also part of *kavvanah*, the special intentions of your *davvenen*.

Then there is *heshbon ha'nefesh*, 'soul-accounting.' Imagine — before Rosh Hashanah my personal 'computer' is running very slow. How am I going to speed it up? *Oy!* So many of the files are fragmented. It is clear that I have to 'defrag' my inner files. What else do I have to do? Well, there are also a lot of 'temp files' that I have to get rid of. They have nothing do with today; they were relevant to something five years ago. So why do I need all these temp files? Then there is the way in which I understand something, that is to say, how it registers in my mind, in my awareness. I have to unscramble the 'registry' too. So I do all these things with my 'computer.'

---

* Rabbi Moshe Hayyim Luzzatto (1707-1743) was an important Italian kabbalist and author of many classic works.

** The mytically oriented prayer service of Rabbi Yitzhak Luria (1534-1572).

Now, in our Life Operating System, for example, a bribe is a 'virus.' The Torah says that we should not take a bribe because it *"blinds the eyes of the wise and twists the words of the righteous."** So I ask myself, "Who is the one who bribes me the most?" *Me.* Imagine I am a senator, and I have to make up my mind about how I am going to vote on healthcare. Every time I try to vote my conscience, something whispers in my ears: *But if you do that, you won't be reelected next year.* This is where the internal 'bribes' come in? It is a *twisting* of one's moral compass. So the 'operating system' of a person's morality can also harbor a 'virus,' and that has to be eliminated.

How do we do that? The best way to do that is to do *Kriyat Sh'ma' Sh'al Ha'Mittah* before boing to sleep, to say the bedtime prayer and review the day, seeing what it was about for you. For that you have to have inner space.

I once heard a young Reform rabbi speak who impressed me a lot. He came to a meeting where there were lots of rabbis and educators talking *at* each other saying, "My way is the right way, and the best way, and you should pay attention what I am saying." Then he got up to speak and he says, "I cannot understand how you can talk and answer so quickly without first taking five minutes to consult your values?" That touched me a lot.

If I can take a moment to consult my values at the beginning of my day, then I will likely be more aware of the possible pitfalls I will encounter in the course of my day. It is not as likely that I will get tripped-up on them because I will remember, "No, I do not want to do that." This is the business of *heshbon ha'nefesh,* consulting our values.

There are a lot of mitzvahs that we can do without our hands or our mouths. We can do thirty-two mitzvahs with consciousness alone.** Just thinking — *God, You are*

---

* Deuteronomy 16:19.

** According to Rabbi Ahron Roth (1894-1944). See my *Ahron's Heart: The Prayers, Teachings and Letters of Ahrele Roth, a Hasidic Reformer.*

One; I have faith in You; I open myself to You; I love you God—only takes a moment of awareness, and yet, fulfills a *mitzvah*.

One of the classic works of the Jewish tradition is *Hovot Ha'levavot,* the 'duties of the heart.' Doing the duties of the heart is another part of Jewish meditation. In the middle of the day, we can always take a moment to do these duties. Some of these might be called 'arrow prayers.' Imagine if I were to set a timer to ring a small bell every quarter of an hour that would remind me to stop and say, "Thank you, *Ribbono shel Olam. Shiviti Ha'Shem L'negdi tamid.* I am aware of You; I am aware of Your Presence."

We are taught that we should "love the LORD our God with what our heart is in."* The sense is that sometimes when we enjoy something, we do not always want anyone to know that we are enjoying it: *It is just for me; it is a secret pleasure.* We really begin to get into this notion after puberty. But is nevertheless important to be able to say to God, "You gave me the opportunity to feel pleasure in this, and I don't want to hide this from You." If I am enjoying something I'm eating, I should be able to say: *"Yum . . . Ribbono shel Olam,* do You like the taste of this chocolate? It is delicious!"

All this goes into *shleymut ha'avodah,* into the way in which we serve.

Following After God

What do we aspire to? There was a man who said, "I try to think of what God must see in me, and that becomes my template." In the same way, I would like t say to God, "God, I need you to pull me toward You." Most of the time, we feel it is our responsibility: *I should . . . I want to . . . I must . . .* What a difference it makes when I feel that God is pulling me to a *mitzvah: Something good is*

---

* Deuteronomy 6:5.

coming up, and I cannot refrain from doing that mitzvah. God is pulling me toward it. That is a *ga'agu'im* meditation, a meditation of my 'longing.' What am I longing for? *I want to be pulled after You, God; take me into Your sanctuary.*

Then there is something else that has to do with 'orientation.' We are told, "You should walk after the LORD your God."* *Aharey Ha'Shem* — 'go behind God,' 'follow God.' I have a sense of endless divine compassion, without which, we wouldn't exist. On the other hand, we have so many questions: *Why are there so many tsores (troubles) in the world?* Who feels the *tsores* of the people? God who is there with them in their pain.

We can go also to that matrix, the Central Heart of Divine Compassion that wants to give goodness to the whole world. Catholics speak of this as the 'Sacred Heart.' We speak of it as the divine name — *Y-H-V-H.* Buddhists speak of Avalokiteshvara, the *bodhisattva* of compassion. To put oneself in the place of that compassion, the heart of compassion, even for a short time — allowing the energy that comes through it to stream through us into the world — that is a great form of meditation and *davvenen.*

Sometimes "following after God" is checking-out what the law, what *halakhah* has to say. It is very clear that, on the basis of all the *halakhot* that we have, if we were to live according to them, we would be closer to sanctity. Of course, some of it has to be updated. For example, my first computer was an Exidy Sorcerer with 36 kilobytes of memory. Now, if I were to try to run a program from that computer on my current computer, nothing would happen. Nevertheless, at the time, I was able to create some very good files on it, to give shape to some good ideas, and with the right conversion software, I can save them on my current computer.

---

* Deuteronomy 13:5.

49

You see, we often have a mistaken notion that God God *gave* us revelation, when actually God is *giving* us revelation, right now, in the present moment. That is why we say, *Barukh attah Ha'Shem* notayn *ha'Torah,* "You give the Torah right now" — it is coming down from heaven at this moment.*

The other day, I opened one of my applications on the computer and immediately a message popped-up saying, "There is an update available." I wish that people could open up the *siddur* in every *shul* and have an immediate update available. Can you imagine what thee updates would have to say about ecology, or social justice? What it would be like if we were prepared to download the update? One of the ways in which we do that is to open ourselves in meditation to hear what kind of 'update' may be coming through — *Asher aniy m'tzavkha ha'yom.*

Sometimes when I see someone doing something beautiful, I call them a *mentsh.* For example, there was a fire in a northern suburb of Boston before Christmas and a factory was burned down. The owner of the factory was a Mr. Feuerstein. Because the factory had burned down in the winter, and during the holiday season for his employees, he told them that he would continue to pay them their wages until the plant reopened. What a *mentsh!* There is something about a person hewing to an ideal that says: *In this person there dwells the Divine will in an active way.*

Then we have the notion, *oto tira'u,* "you shall fear" God.** People are often confused by the words, "fear God"; but it is not raw fear. Sometimes people translate it as 'awe,' but that's actually a higher rung, *Yir'at Haromemut.* So imagine someone comes into a room. They think there is no one else there, and perhaps they pass gas. It is a normal function of the body, right? But we don't want

---

* From the daily liturgy, the blessing on the Torah.

** Deuteronomy 13:5.

to do it in public. Thinking nobody else is there, they do it without shame. All of a sudden, they realize that someone else is standing there in the room with them, and they have a startle reflex — *I have been seen!* The Hebrew *ra'oh,* 'to see,' is related *yir'ah,* 'fear,' to be inspected.

Jacob, our father, finds himself in a situation when he says, *Akhen yesh Y-H-V-H bamakom hazzeh va'anokhi lo yada'ti,* "Look, there is God and I didn't know it."* *Akhen attah Eyl mistater,* "Here You are the hiding God."** We are not talking about fearing in the sense of terror or being afraid, but rather, becoming aware that I am *being seen.* It is so important to install this program in our constant-awareness; it is one of the keys to the mindfulness that we call 'living deliberately' and with *kavvanah.* That is what the *shiviti* gazing device of the divine name is trying to achieve.***

If you look long enough at a Hindu *yantra* (a geometric diagram of a divine quality), all of a sudden it seems that the representation is melting away and you're in the land of the heart's imagination. That is what the *shiviti* is trying to do for us. That is also why I like to light candles before I start to *davven.* I do this even during the week, because the live candle suggests that it is a sacrificial offering I am making. That prepares us to surrender the ego so that the sacred flow can move through us.

There is so much more to say.

There is a beautiful sentence in the Psalms that says, "I was just a beast" — like an animal without awareness, like a *behemah* — "with You." Nevertheless, "I am always

---

* Genesis 28:16.

** Isaiah 45:15.

*** A device prominenty featuring the letters of the divine name, *Y-H-V-H,* often surrounded by significant verses, sometimes forming symbols from the Jewish tradition, such as a *menorah.*

with You, and You have taken hold of my right hand."* There is a great sense of *d'veikut* in that.

A *b'rakhah:* may you be blessed with good meditations. *V'nomar: Amen.*

Question and Answer Session

Question: In the beginning you were saying that sometimes we are not visible to God.

Reb Zalman: How do you think I mean it?

Response: "Where can we go from Your Spirit; where can we hide from Your Presence?"** You always see us. Maybe it is that *we* think we are hiding.

Reb Zalman: I am more worried about the psychological aspect. In *Star Trek,* they are always saying, "Activate the cloaking device." There are times when I do not want God to see me.

Response: So *I* am hiding.

Reb Zalman: Right. In that case, it is not that God doesn't see me. *Im yastir Ish b'mistarim — va-ani lo er'enu?* "If a person is going to hide himself, will I not see him?"*** At the same time, there is that moment in which we do not want to be seen. That is what I meant.

Response: I see a little kid closing his eyes and saying, "You can not see me".

---

* Psalms 73:22-23.

** Psalms 139:7.

*** Jeremiah 23:24.

Reb Zalman: Exactly, exactly that—yes.

Question: So that willingness to be vulnerable is the opening of the eyes and allowing yourself to be seen.

Reb Zalman: Look, there are so many things . . .

I used to do those I-Thou labs with people. We would look one another in the eye for quite a while *to see each other* and then comes a moment when we each get scared: *They are going to see everything inside me; I don't want them to see it.* That is the moment I have to be able to say to God, "But *You* can; I'll let You see me. I remove that barrier. I know that wasn't such a nice thing that I did, and I didn't want You to see it, but am I stupid? I cannot hide it from You."

There is a wonderful story of Reb Mikheleh Zlotchover who could read your sins on your forehead.* A Hassid comes to see him with his hat over his forehead. The Rebbe says, "Fool, do you think that if I can see what's on your forehead, I couldn't see through your hat?"

Question: You spoke of creating "a window for God"— can you speak a little more about that?

Reb Zalman: Imagine you're talking with someone on the telephone and sharing secrets, and you hear a click and you know someone else picked up the phone. You get a sense of being overheard, right? It is the same kind of the thing. You walk into a room and you notice a spy camera there, and you know you are being seen. This has to do with our consciousness. The whole notion of having a secret that nobody can know is disappearing in this digital age. We spy on each other. We have to learn to live with being seen. That is the only way the world is going to come together. If everyone were morally *unshielded,*

---

* Rabbi Yehiel Mikheleh of Zlotchov (1731-1786), a disciple of the Ba'al Shem Tov.

naked, visible to everyone else, can you imagine how governments would be much better? Most people do not open such a window.

Question: Do you feel open all the time? Do you hear the "click" and feel that someone is listening all the time?

Reb Zalman: Often when I have a session with an individual or with a goup of people, I remind them that, "This call is being monitored for quality purposes." It is not something that is so private. But, if you ask me, "Am I always like this?" *No!*

Look, God doesn't mind that I use the bathroom, right? Do I want to be observed by God even then? There are people who say, "You should not think holy thoughts in the bathroom," but I don't think it is wrong. It is natural. But "All the time?" No . . . no. After using the bathroom, we say the *b'rakhah, Asher Yatzar—galuy v'yadu'a* and declare that we are transparent to God.

Question: You feel the partnership?

Reb Zalman: I always have to remind myself to work on that. If anybody says they *"have it"* without having to work on it, I don't know if I believe them.

I'll tell you a funny story.

This is a story about a Hasid of the Tzanzer Rebbe.* He was making his way back from visiting his Rebbe and coming to a little town where he stays for *Shabbat* as a guest of the local rabbi. On Sunday, when he's about to leave, the local rabbi says to him, "Why do you have to go all the way to Tzanz? You could come to me; I could also be your teacher."

---

* Rabbi Hayyim Halberstam of Tzanz (1797-1876), a disciple of the Seer of Lublin and Naftali of Ropshitz.

The Hasid says, "Because in Tzanz I learned how to read minds."

"*Hah!*" he says. "So tell me what I am thinking."

"You are thinking, *Shiviti Ha'Shem l'negdi tamid.*"

"No, I'm not."

"That's why I go to Tzanz, because *my* Rebbe *is* always thinking *Shiviti Ha'Shem l'negdi tamid.*"

Fourth Talk
Gratitude and Self-Examination

The *tallit* I wear in prayer has blue threads in the *tzitzit*. The person who rediscovered the blue thread *(tekhelet)* — allowing us to observe the commandment as it is written in the Torah — was a man by the name of Reb Gershon Hanokh of Radzhin (grandson of the Izhbitzer). Today is his *yahrzeit*, the anniversary of his death.* I so appreciate him and the work that he did against blind and stubborn opposition, and I would like him to be my ally in presenting this material to you.

A Grateful Mentality

Some people tell me: *"Oy! I wish I could pray. I'm just not able to get into prayer; it's too much for me. How do you have to be in order to pray right?"* With these people, I often share the *Modeh Ani:* "I give thanks to You, living and eternal King, for having returned my soul to me; great is Your faithfulness." In other words — *I'm grateful that You have entrusted me with another day of life.*

Sometimes I put it this way: "Dear God, I see that You want to be Zalman for yet another day? Okay, I'll do my best to give You a good ride." Prayer that begins with gratitude is just easier. When you allow yourself to feel the life of your entire body — from your toes up through your torso, breathing into all of its regions — realizing how wonderful it is to take a breath and feel your heartbeat, it is pretty easy to be grateful.

---

* Rabbi Gershon Hanokh Leiner of Radzhin (1839-1891) was the grandson of Rabbi Mordecai Yosef of Izhbitz.

A grateful mentality is a prerequisite for prayer. How can a grumpy person do more than *kvetch?* I am not saying that you shouldn't pray to God when you have problems. After all, to whom else can you go when the going is tough? Who else is going to give you that kind of ear and desire to help? I am talking about prayer and spiritual work in general, not so much about praying for a particular thing. Here is where you can come with an openness of heart and an optimism that says, *Barukh sh'amar v'hayah ha'olam,* "Thank you God! You spoke and there was the world."* When you begin with this attitude, or with something like the *Modeh Ani* thanksgiving, everything begins to go better.

There is something else about cultivating gratitude that goes a little deeper. Remember when I was talking about the lonely place within us? That place, deep in the heart, from which we exclude everbody except God — the place of which we make a sanctuary for God, the place of our intimate tryst with God — *that* is the best place for prayer. Even if you are in the best and biggest *shul,* with the greatest number of people, if you don't log-on from that sanctuary, the likelihood is that you will just be going through the motions, spinning your wheels in the pew. So it is important to go into that sacred place.

Most people are unaware of the fact that, in infinitesimal nano-seconds, the universe opens up for every creature, and it is in that moment that we are One with God. But it is happening so fast that we aren't really conscious of it.

Imagine someone has a very slow film and is trying to take a picture at 1,000th of a second shutter speed. The likelihood is that they won't get anything clear on film. It is not sensitive enough; the shutter speed was too fast to receive the image.

---

* *Barukh She'amar* in the daily liturgy.

The Talmud says that every day a heavenly voice issues from Sinai asking us, "Children, return!" to remind us who we really are, deep inside.* Can you imagine what it would be like if we had a way of keeping the aperture open longer, so that instead of 1,000th of a second we could hold it open for a whole second, and for that second we would have prepared a sensitive container in our heart, taking a snapshot of our oneness with God? If I have that, I can live as a vital soul in a vital body.

When you become aware that this is happening at all times, although we haven't a way to dilate that opening for us, then you see why it is necessary for us to meditate, to contemplate, because that prepares our sensitivity, and also makes the 'shutter' stay open a small bit longer.

Therefore, I want to make sure that you will be really careful to allow a deep gratitude to be active in you. When that happens, that very tiny flash of which we are unconscious, burrows its way into our awareness, and that is what makes it so much easier and better for us to stay commited to God, because that commitment demands a deep unitary awareness.

Biblical Meditation

In my previous talk, I spoke about what is specifically *Jewish* in Jewish meditation. Sometimes people ask me, "What does the Bible say about meditation?" And I want to quote from Torah, *V'yada'ata ha'yom — v'hashevota al l'vavvekha ki Y-H-V-H hu ha'Elohim bashamyim mima'al v'al ha'aretz mitahat — eyn od*, "And you shall know today, and take it to heart, that Y-H-V-H is God, in heaven above and earth below, and nothing else exists."**

Now, how do I get to that knowing? By opening my awareness to *Y-H-V-H* is *Elohim*. What does that mean?

---

* Talmud, Hagigah 15a.

** Deuteronomy 4:39.

Very few people have any problem saying that, if there is a universe, there is a source for the universe, and the source of the universe we call God. In Hebrew we use the name *Elohim*. The numerical value the name *Elohim* is 86, which is exactly the numerical value to the word *hateva'*, nature. So when the philospher Barukh Spinoza says, *Deus sive Natura*, God equals nature, that was his way of saying that they are identical; but that is not the God to whom we can pray.*

This is the big problem, because the God who creates the laws of nature also makes things poisonous. It is somewhat problematic to say the God of nature, "You should be kind to us." So who is the God we are talking to? *Y-H-V-H* in whose Image we are made. Consider, our head is like the *Yud*, our arms and shoulders like the *Heh*, the trunk of our body like the *Vav*, the pelvis and legs like the other *Heh*.

That is a *personal* God, a personally relatable God. This bothers some people who feel that they have abandoned the personal God for an impersonal monistic notion of divinity; but the heart is not satisfied with a philosophical concept, a divine abstraction. The heart wants to have a feeling and caring presence with whom to relate. This is why Martin Buber spoke of two ways of approaching the world. He called these "primary words," underlying all perception and speech. One is *I-It*—I the person relating to an object, a thing. The other is *I-Thou*—I the person relating to another person recognized in their utter uniquness.** I don't know what that person is going to do, or say, or think; I have to

---

* Baruch Spinoza (1632-1677) was a philosopher of Portuguese Jewish origin.

** Martin Buber (1878-1965) was a German-Jewish philosopher and author of the classic, *I and Thou*.

going to do, or say, or think; I have to relate to them as a unique center of consciousness with an integrity of their own. Likewise, when I'm praying, I don't want to feel that I'm talking to the wall; I want to be able to address the compassionate *heart* of God. And this, according to our tradition, is what is signified by name Y-H-V-H.

Now let's bring these two views together, as if with stereoscopic vision. On one side of my contemplative mind, I can *see* the *I-Thou* God, and on the other, I can see the God of nature, the God who is permeates and obliterates everything that we know. Now, the mouth, being a serial instrument, cannot say two different things at once. But the eyes can bring two visions together in a whole.

If you can bring together the God ideas that have to do with a God with whom you can relate and talk, who loves and cares for you, *and* the God of nature, seeing them as One, then you have done the kind of meditation the Torah recommends.

But we still have to consider how to achieve this? So the Torah says: *Attah har'eta lada'at ki Y-H-V-H hu ha'Elohim eyn od mil'vado,* "You have made Yourself visible to us" — so we could see that this isn't only an idea that *we* put together, so we could see that — "nothing else exists except You."* It is not a contradiction; it is a paradox for a higher level of awareness.

When you see that truly, *you* tend to disappear momentarily; but soon you return to the body with a more integrated vison of yourself, God, and the world.

The problem is that sometimes the ego says, *"Oy!* Am I a good meditator! Look at how *I* put it all together!" But at that point the vision has become an *object* that you have created as 'a great meditation artist.' "Look at the profound ideas I have conceived." I no longer feel that I am being *seen* by God, because I am in my ego-space; *I* am the subject, and the idea that I was thinking about,

---

* Deuteronomy 4:35.

61

God, is but an *object,* an artifact of my thinking. When people face an artifact and think of it as divine, they have created an idol.

But what if I said: "Oh God! Look at these ideas in my head; they're all about You—I love You!" See what a difference that makes? Because, at that point, you can be open in your heart, you can be more vulnerable. The ego doesn't take as much credit, because the center is acknowledged to be in God. *Va'anhnu kor'im,* "We bow down and kneel before You the King of Kings, the holy One blessed be He."* That is to say, *You are the center and we are on the periphery.*

But there are also healthy doubts that creep up and say: "*Oy!* You think you're already there? Sure, you've got good ideas, and you always talk big about what a person *ought to do;* but what about how you *really are?* There's quite a discrepancy between your *ought* and your *is,* and this is your problem."

Once, the King of the Khazars was looking for a religion to call his own and asked a Christian teacher, a Muslim, and philosopher to speak about their religion to him, but he wasn't satisfied with what they had to say. For all their talk, they could not interpret the meaning of a recurring dream that plagued him: *Your intention is good, but how you are living is not.* That is the discrepancy between the *is* and the *ought.*

Unfortunately, it is also easy to get discouraged—"I am so far from my *ought."* Sometimes cynicism makes me say, "I don't want to deal with that." But if I allow the pull of longing, the pull of disappointment with my *is* to touch me, so that I feel that I really want to live according to my *ought*—that is wonderful.

I have often called my friend, Reb Shlomo Carlebach, peace be upon him, as a "genius of *virtuous* reality," because he would tell stories in such a way that people

---

* *Aleinu,* in the daily liturgy.

were usually inspired to live a more virtuous lie afterward. He created a pull, a longing for us to become better. *Oy!* Wouldn't it be wonderful if every time we were in *shul* the people who read the Torah would do so in such a way that it was opened up for us and we could say, "I'd like to live that way . . . Would that it were so"? That is why, sometimes when I lead prayer and we come to the *Sh'ma'*, I ask the people to say in between the word groups, *Halevay!* 'Would that it were so.' So we would recite, "Thou shalt love the Lord your God with all your heart and all your soul with all your might—*Halevay!*" When I say, "*Halevay!*" I invite it to pull me to a greater level of *ought*.

Where did we get our great *ought?* We were just out of Egypt, just rabble working in the clay pits—not even blue-collar workers—we leave Egypt, and within 49 days, we are at Mt. Sinai and receiving an enormous *OUGHT*, one that says this is the way a person ought to be. Why is that? Because *Anokhi Y-H-V-H Elokekha!* We heard God pronounce the "*I Am*" reverberating through all of existence. There was this flash of divinity and caring coming through for us, which was saying, "I want to have a covenant with you," and then the door opened for us! That is why we call this *Mattan Torah* and *Kabbalat ha'Torah*—the *giving* of the Torah on God's part, and the *receiving* of the Torah on our part—which makes it possible for us to think about how we may become what we ought to be.

Reprise: What is Meditation?

Lets review something else I spoke about earlier. I really want to make sure these ideas take root in you.

Perhaps a meditation is a daydream, a daydream of the Soul as the Beloved and G-d, the Lover— their meeting in the tryst of prayer, their yearning for one another after parting, a daydream of their being united again.

When did you last have a romantic daydream about God? Such daydreams are very important! For instance, it is Friday afternoon, and you start singing *Shir Ha'Shirim:* "Oh let him kiss me with the kisses of his mouth—for your loving is better than wine."* These beautiful words of King Solomon's speak of a romantic relationship, and the Midrash is full of images of God as the King courting Israel and the *Shekhinah*. So the day-dream is about meeting in the tryst of prayer, and the yearning for one another after parting, and another day-dream of being united again. If the embrace were contin-ual, it wouldn't be as delicious. For each time it is re-newed, that feeling rushes back in with intensity.

> Or perhaps a meditation is the human soul becoming aware of its loneliness and anticipating its being united with the One Who transcends the all and conquers one's defences.

Like the songs say: "Nobody knows the troubles I've seen" and "Sometimes I feel like a motherless child." Where do I go when I'm in that place? Even my best friend can't quite know everything that I want him to know about me. So I have to go into that very special place of solitude, into the loneliness. But in there is the anticipation of being united with the One who transcends all, who sees all and is able to pass one's own defenses, to whom we say: *"Oy! Ribbono shel Olam,* I want to let You in; I want You to break the door down!

> Or perhaps, again, it is a standing back with the whole of the cosmos before one's mind's eye as the heart is filled with the sheer joy of seeing the balance of the All and one's own self as part of it.

---

* Song of Songs 1:2.

Can you imagine this? Even now we are getting background radiation from the Big Bang! There is now a new Hubble telescope — How far you can see with it?

Imagine you are sitting down, wrapped in your *tallit*, and looking at the whole panorama of the sky, so that it is like a planetarium in your head. When is it time for that imagery in the *davvenen?* When we say *Barkhu* and talk about the angels, the *Serafim*, the galaxies, the signs of the Zodiac, and the *Ofanim*, the cycling planets!

But it is not only in the conceptual mind, it is also in one's heart, which is "filled with the sheer joy of seeing the balance of the All and one's own self as part of it." To be graced to see this wonderful vastness, becoming aware that I am integral to it — what a joy that is!

Or perhaps it is a searching into one's own motives, values and wishes, with the light of the Torah against the background of the past.*

What do I really want? What is my hierarchy of needs? What are my priorities? I check these out and say, "Is that the way I ought to be? Is that the way the Torah wants me to be? Is that God's picture of me?"

Steering the Mind

I want to return to the subject of 'steering the mind' for a moment. Most of the time, we just sit back and let our minds do what they want. But sometimes we want to think about particular things, and sometimes we want to keep it from thinking about things. The question is — How do we take hold of the mind's steering wheel? That is where *kavvanah* comes in.

Again, the basic meaning of *kavvanah* has to do with aiming at a target. What is my target? Imagine I would

---

* All of these passages are drawn from the section, "What is Meditation?" in my book, *Gate to the Heart: An Evolving Process.*

like to be able to recite the words of the first section of the *Sh'ma'*, and not have any other thoughts intrude upon my recitation. Try it and see what happens. You almost need a flyswatter to swat all the thoughts that want to be heard. So *kavvanah* is like the track you lay down for your mind to follow upon. It is not so different from when we have to make important decisions, and we say, "I need to figure this one out," and then begin to plan and lay the track from milepost to milepost.

Another method of *kavvanah* is stilling the mind and simply observing one's thoughts. While this is most often associated with Buddhist meditation, it was also advocated by a Hasidic master, Reb Kalonymus Kalmish of Piasetzno, who suggested:

> "A person is to look at his thoughts for a small amount of time—say a few minutes—and then begin to see how slowly his mind is emptying and his thoughts stop rushing in their usual manner. Then let him begin to say one phrase such as *'Ribbono Shel Olam'* " in order to connect his mind with one thought of holiness [. . .] It is also possible to achieve the stilling by making use of a watch, looking at it for some time; this too will calm the flow of constantwanting and the rushingof the mind. Then, when the mind is calm, that brings about the indwelling from above.*

If the background noise in the mind hasn't abated, it's very hard to be able to follow through with any interior work.

How does one begin to make that space? Very few people have carved out enough inner space in themselves in this form of meditation. These are the ways in which

---

* This passage is translated in my book, *Gate to the Heart: An Evolving Process*.

we strengthen our steering muscles, so that can stay on target with our *kavvanah*.

Wholeness in the Service of God

Among the things that make up the matrix on which all this is supposed to happen is *shleymut ha'avodah*. As I said before, Moshe Hayyim Luzatto spoke of this in his *Mesillat Yesharim*. In this, he also said: I don't have anything new to tell you. I am just going to tell you what you already know, but tend to ignore and don't do much about. You set it aside, always wanting something new. But I'm here to remind you of what you already know.

So Reb Moshe Hayyim says the most important religious act in Judaism is *shleymut ha'avodah*, 'completeness,' or 'wholeness in the service of God.' Look at all the extrinsic motivations that we have when we come to a *shul* — socializing, prestige, dating — we think about everything else, but not so much about *shleymut ha'avodah*, not so much about placing ourselves in the Presence of the living God.

At least once a day, we need to re-calibrate ourselves to be able to say, "Look, serving God isn't only *davvenen*, isn't only meditating, it is also driving your car, eating, and taking care of your bodily needs." All this is in the service of God. But keep in mind that you want to do this in such a way that the *quality* will reach the level of *shleymut ha'avodah*, of wholeness in the service of God. When that is there, then every form of meditation is okay, because what you are doing is making yourself transparent to God, removing the opacity projected by my ego, and saying: There isn't anything that I don't want to show to God."

That leads us to *heshbon*, the examination of conscience.

Now let's get back to our discussionon how to move from *is* to *ought*. Sometimes during the week we say *Tahanun*, the 'supplication' section in the prayer book. It is a way of saying: "Dear God, help me to do it better. Forgive me for what I need forgiveness for." But it isn't only for begging forgiveness; it is also saying, "What can I do to prevent the same mistakes again?" And that is one of the most difficult things in the world. Why? Because every one of us is created with a little flaw, as in Reb Nahman's story of the candelabra.

Once, a man sent his son to apprentice in the art of making candelabras. And he learned to make them beautifully. So when he finally came home, his father said to him, "Would you please show us what you have learned and make us a candelabra that I can show off to the people?" The son agreed to do it, but instead of going straight into the workshop, he began to visit the people of the town, and spent time talking with each of them. After a while, he came back and started making the candelabra.

The father says, "It is very beautiful, wonderful, but what is this — it doesn't look quite right?" He had found a flaw. His son is silent. Then the father takes the candelabra and shows it around to everyone, and everyone thinks it is beautiful, but each of them finds something wrong with the candelabra.

So the father comes home ashamed, saying, "My son, my son, I thought it was beautiful, but everyone I showed it to found some flaw." So the son says, "Papa, both you and they are right; this candelabra was made entirely of flaws. I went and talked to everyone in order to discover their flaws and I built this candelabra from them."

What does this mean? We each have our own personal flaws, our own personal blind spots, and it is difficult to manage a blind spot. You have to have a good friend who will keep you on track, who will keep you aware of your blind spot. In this way, sometimes you can get a glimpse of it before it tries to hide itself again.

When it does manage to hide itself again, what happens is that you repeat a mistake. You may say, "I'm not going to make that mistake again," but in one way or another, you *will* make that mistake again. It is the same old bride under a new veil.

Imagine you have a leak in your gas tank, and it's going to cause you some trouble. If you know there is a leak, maybe you can do something about it. In the same way, you might wonder: *How is my spirituality leaking away from me?* When I recognize the flaw, I can factor it in to my decisions. At the end of the day when I sit back and I ask what was my day about, I can start looking for the strategies to make fewer mistakes in that direction.

There will always be certain things that are characteristic of a person. Moshe *rabbeinu* remains Moshe *rabbeinu* until his dying day, and Ahron and remains Ahron to his dying day. Until Moshe *rabbeinu*'s dying day there was no problem with his body, which was kept well and healthy. For all the changes in his life and his great experiences, he was the same character. So you see, we are discussing the characterological substance in which the flaw is embedded. Therefore we have to watch out for this when we do *heshbon ha'nefesh* before going to sleep.

The Texture of Time

If I could actually *see* all that is going on here — microwaves, cell phone and radio signals, everything that is going through this space at this time — I would be caught in a fantastic stream of messages. And depending on what I would attune myself to, the message I receive would be different. That is what my radio does for me; it tunes into that wavelength that I want.

Many people don't realize that time has texture. Mondays are often a little blue and weighty. God didn't say, "It was good" on Monday. Tuesday is happier because God twice said, "It is good."* Everyday has texture, *Shabbat* having the finest and most subtle texture. Imagine time is like a stream—How do I best navigate down the stream of time? This is a real question. When I know *Shabbat* is coming, then I begin to 'navigate' *Shabbesdik*.

Likewise, when Pesah is coming, I navigate in that direction, because the calendar is important. It helps us to touch the 'chakras' inside of the Jewish soul and to stabilize it in her journey. So on Yom Kippur I connect with that energy and straighten-out my *Keter*, the highest level of spiritual energy within me. On Rosh Hashanah, I take care of my *Hokhmah* and *Binah*, my intellectual apparatus. Pesah is *Hesed*, my kindness. Shavuot is *Gevurah*, my toughness. Sukkot is *Tiferet*, my heart. Purim is *Netzah*, the victory in my right leg, as it were, and Hanukkah is *Hod*, the glory in my left leg. Rosh Hodesh is *Yesod*, the foundation of the genitals, and *Shabbat* is *Malkhut*, my kingdom, my basis, the ground on which I stand.

Once you get a notion that time has texture, you know that it is important to be able to navigate according to the time. If this is the time for sadness and I try to be happy, it will not get me anywhere.

There are some people think you should never be sad. On Tish'ah B'av one has to be sad. There were some people who used to wake up in the middle of the night and weep for the exile of the Divine Presence. It's a beautiful world, but nobody recognizes the one to whom the world belongs. They don't see the presence of God. So people would cry over that tragedy and be sad.

It is important to know what to do with the sadness. For there is *sour* sadness called *atzvut* (sadness), which is self-pitying and always sees itself as the poor abused vic-

---

* Genesis 1:9-13.

tim. Then there is a *bitter* sadness called *m'rirut* (bitterness), which protests: "I won't have it anymore! I'll do something about it." There are definitely times for *atzvut;* if I don't feel the sadness, I won't feel the joy either. The heart has to be open for both. If you block the feelings on one side, you also block the feelings on the other side.

But I also want to tell you about the different kinds of time. There is 'commodity time' and there is 'organic time.' In commodity time, you count 60 minutes on the clock; but if you go to organic time, you get a sense of how much energy and awareness is in that time. If I were a psychologist, I would have to charge the people who came from 10:00 to 11:00 AM three times as much as those who came from 2:00 to 3:00 PM. The quality of my mind-space is just better in the morning, more clear.

An awareness of the texture of time is a contribution that Judaism makes to the world. I am very proud of this, because no other culture has such a way of organizing organic time considering the natural cycles. Pesah is always at the full moon of the vernal equinox, and Sukkot is always on the full moon of the autumnal equinox. This points to the harmonizing of the solar and lunar calendars, allowing us to live in organic time.

Nevertheless, the world likes to deal in commodity time. 'Time is money.' We pay a certain amount per hour, and we rarely talk about *quality.* Once a week, it is really necessary for us is to be able to step out of commodity time and say, *Yom ha'shishi* and sanctify the *Shabbat* in organic time for the next 26 hours.

Kol tuv (all good) to you.

Question and Answer Session

Question: How will you know if you are doing it right?

71

Reb Zalman: Fortunately for us, God created empiricism. Remember when we you were a child and you played 'hot and cold'? "You're getting warmer and warmer and warmer . . ." That is feedback. Anything that is alive gives us a certain amount of feedback. I also have a sense that there are holy 'endorphins.' There is a way in which the body releases a chocolate-like chemical into our feeling-field that makes us feel good. *"Oy!* was this a good *davvenen!"* This is how you know.

There are other things that are the more difficult. *Oy!* If I were able to find a litmus test for the tongues of our senators, to see if their motives in their speeches are intrinsic and honest; when they talk about healthcare, are they really talking about being re-elected next year? What is really going on? To what extent are you bribing yourself? This is difficult, but we try to discriminate and ask ourselves, "Am I on the right track? Part of my motivation is that I want to that extrinsic thing, so it makes me feel I'm doing right one moment, and I'm on track. But is it really with my *ought* in the right place?" It's not easy. If I had an easy method to offer, I would offer it gladly.

Question: On a related note, you said that we have "holy endorphins." There are times when I do something, and I know it's the right thing to do, but it feels really bad temporarily. Ultimately, it feels good; but I get confused when I do something that has holy endorphins and I also feel good. Sometimes I think only holy things should feel hard, so I get confused when holy things actually feel good, and think that maybe this is my ego that wants to do this — it's not really a holy endorphin.

Reb Zalman: This is why we have to do the inner work. For instance, when I'm doing it, I may not be aware of the hidden motives that I have for doing it. But then comes the evening and I look over the day, scrutinizing my motives while I face God; I give thanks for what was good during the day, and I look over what was not so good and decide to make *tikkun*, a 'correction' the next day. I pray for the people I've met during the day, and having done that, I can yield myself up to God's love during the night in the most restful way, into God's everlasting arms.

Fifth Talk
Keva and Kavvanah[*]

Once the Holy Temple in Jerusalem was immensely important to us. By connecting with it, we were able to recalibrate ourselves to be in the right place spiritually, aligned with God and the divine will. So there must have been something more to it than stones and wood, gold and silver. What was it? I believe it was an accumulator and dispensor of spiritual energy. Each sacrifice offered there, every song the Levites sang, added to the power available at the Temple for our sacred use.

The Rabbis said, "He who worked before the *Shabbat* to prepare for *Shabbat* will eat on *Shabbat*."[**] If you want your prayer to be answered, you have to invest in the prayer pool, in the *God-field*.

Earlier, I discussed the *I-Thou* relationship with God. We have to understand something: the mind that holds the universe in existence, wants to communicate with us continually.

Imagine I am sending you an electronic message, but your computer doesn't have a way to put this into an ASCII formula, an alphabet that you can read. My important message would never even show up on your screen. So it is necessary for me to know what kind of message my recipient can handle. In the same way, we are the typewriters, the printers, through which God sends messages: *Dibra Torah bil'shon Adam*, "Torah speaks in the

---

[*] *Keva* and *Kavvanah*: structure, the fixed prayer tradition; and intentionality, the prayer of the heart.

[**] Talmud, Avodah Zarah 3a.

language of human beings."* This is to say, the particular expression of the message depends on the time and place in history, on what the technology and understanding was at that time.

There was an American linguist-philosopher by the name of Korzybski (who was a founder of semantics) and he said that in order to understand the meaning of a word in context, the word needs a "time-binder."** For example, if I say the word 'freedom' in the year 2,448 B.C.E., I am talking about the Exodus from Egypt. If I say 'freedom' in 1776 C.E., I am talking about a different kind of freedom. So the words used in divine communication with us have something to do in the way in which we handle language and what it means to us.

Look at the prayer book, the *siddur*, it's like a museum; it contains biblical, rabbinic, medieval, and renaissance material. It's not quite current, because eligion has a way of being a step behind the current technology. Priests of all traditions have worn garments which the rest of the population no longer wore. In this way, their liturgical garments pointed to the mythological past they represented. When people wore cloaks, the priests wore loincloths. When people wore loincloths, the priests went naked. Tradition has always liked going back one paradigm. Similarly, art is often reaching back into earlier technologies. Instead of using a digital camera, you use a canvas, paint, and brushes.

In recreation too, we often leave the current technology and go back to an earlier one. Hunting with a bow and arrow becomes the sport of in archery. Horseback riding is not so much for transportation as it is for recreation and sports. We sail more for enjoyment than to cross the waters. In each case, I am reaching back to an obsolete technology for the fun and the immediacy of it. The

---

* Talmud, Sanhedrin 90b.

** Alfred Korzybski (1879-1950), a Polish born philosopher and linguist.

current technology tends to distance us from involvement with the body.

In the same way, our liturgy has some archaic elements in it. These connect us to our ancestors and impress subtle influences upon us. We sing melodies that arouse echoes of our ancestors in us. Values accumulated by them awaken in us as we sing those melodies. Without history as an anchor, we are bound to lose our place in the present.

At the same time, if you look at a tree, the history of the tree is in the rings of the wood. But that wood is not quite living anymore; the life of the tree depends on the growing edge beneath the bark. If you peel this off, you kill the tree.

Tradition—and you can observe this in the *siddur*—is what gives the tree structure, substance, and strength, but the *vitality* is in the growing edge. Every religion needs to have a renewal every year, a new growing edge. But it also needs the substance of its history and tradition. If a tree only had the growing edge, the first wind would knock it down. We have to have a past *and* a present in order to have a future.

In prayer, the important question is: Whom do you want to address? *Zeh Eli*, this is my God, *v'anvehu*, the one with whom I have my personal relationship, or the God of my forbears, *Elohey avi va'arom'menu*, whom I will exalt.

There some people who can't make it beyond the God of tradition. They haven't had access to personal experiences of the divine, so they say: "I have to do it just like my father did it. I have to say all the prayers exactly as they have been said before, otherwise I am not fulfilling my obligation. I am not *yotze*." For some people, this is a necessity, and even others who have had personal experiences this is still valid: "I will do this exactly like my father did because this is for my spiritual discipline, and I need my discipline." There is much to be said for sacred routine.

Professor Abraham Joshua Heschel had a good way of talking about this. He would tell the following parable:

There was a small town that had had no watchmaker. When they needed to repair their watches, they had to wait for the watchmaker to come to town. When he came, he would charge two different prices. For those who wound their watches everyday, even though they didn't keep the right time, he charged less. Those who did not wind their watches at all, he charged more. This was because the watches that had been wound everyday, even though not keeping time, were easier to repair.

Therefore, every morning when you're *davvenen,* even if it's routine, like winding the watch, this is good; it will make it easier to fix any issues you are having in your *davvenen.* That is also dealing with *Elohey Avi va'arom'menhu,* my father's God.

A lot of what my parents deposited into that God-space is spiritual 'capital' that I can draw on. This is why we speak of *Z'khut Avot,* 'parental merit.' It gives us energy, the strength that keeps us together when the wind blows hard upon us.

Some days I find that I am so tired it feels as if I have no growing edge. So what do I do? I say to myself, "Today I will just *davven* the *siddur,* because I am tired; I cannot free myself to go higher." But on other days ,when I am, thank God, more focused and energized, I invest more deeply and juice myself up. I will meditate on "this is my God," and let it take me where it is going to take me.

Let me spell this one out; this is so beautiful and important. Rabbi Emanuel Rackman, *alav ha'shalom,* translated the words *Yatza y'dey hovato* as "he extricated himself from the grasp of obligation."* Now take a look at how this appears in life. Many people look upon obligations as burdens: *Okay, I've done it already! You can't have a lien on me anymore.* So he was saying that he had extricated himself from that burden. It is really important for us to extricate ourselves from the sense of being burdened by these things, from the negative connotation, and to do them with a renewed sense of freedom.

Imagine what it would be like to do that same thing for your beloved? Sometimes when I talk about preparing for *Shabbat,* I use this example. Imagine your boss is coming for dinner at six o'clock. By 5:30, every dish is in its right place, the forks, spoons, and knives; everything is set, and you leave it alone. You won't touch it again, so as not to disturb its perfection. But what if it is your beloved that is coming to dinner? You are never are quite satisfied with the arrangement. You move this a little bit, arrange the flowers again to look better. Even when it's all done, it is never finished, because it's not an obligation. You don't have a sense of obligation. You come from a really devotional, generous, and loving place: *What more can I do out of love? How can I offer more to my God for all the boons that have been given to me?*

If I feel obligated to do a *mitzvah,* I will do it meticulously, and then be glad that I'm done with it. But, if I am doing it out of generous and loving devotion, I will add special details of care and beauty. This is what the tradition calls *hiddur mitzvah,* to adorn the *mitzvah.*

When you are feeling gratitude over the grace coming down to you, it is inappropriate to pressure yourself to say every word in the *siddur* as an obligation. That grace is a gift, not something that you worked for, and it should be met with joyful freedom.

---

* Rabbi Emanuel Rackman (1910-2008) was a congregational rabbi in America and later chancellor of Bar-Ilan University.

The question is 'public policy': *Won't this lead to anarchy? Can everyone 'call the shots' for themselves? What about the cohesion of the community?*

In *Klal Yisrael*, the entire body of Jews, there are plenty of people upholding the obligation; but there are very few who are praying spontaneously from the heart. In the end, it has to be stated that this *kavvanah* is also important. In fact, the prayers of the *siddur* wouldn't even exist if someone hadn't gotten enthused and prayed spontaneously, "God, You were King before there was a world . . ."* From that came something new to recite, *halleluyah!* But when you are not receiving that grace, then you do what you have to do, and follow through with the prayers of the *siddur*.

Sometimes when I don't feel like *davvenen* in Hebrew, I pull out a *siddur* that has been translated into another language. It is so wonderful to express your love for God in French—*Beni es Tu Seigneur*; or when I desire grandeur, to go to a *siddur* in Spanish—*Bueno es El Senor a los limpios de Corazon*. If I want theological precision, I can go to a German translation—*Der Atem aller Lebenden ruehmt Deinen Heiligen Namen*. It is wonderful to have access to the words of prayer in other languages. With each I take away another veil from the text, going into the nuances of another language.**

The Divine Metaphor

Now I want to go back to the notion of the God-space. In the past, when people were looking at the way in which the universe is governed, operates, people would speak about it in terms of a ruling Majesty—

---

* *Adon Olam*, one of the great poems of the Jewish tradition, and often included in the liturgy.

** I once read a science fiction story that put it this way: if you have to do science, do it in German; if you want to do romance, do it in French; if you want to do politics, do it in English.

Melekh malkhey ha'm'lokhim ha'kadosh barukh hu. God, the blessed and holy one, is the ruler over kings.

Where did this notion come from? In ancient Israel, King Solomon was a king over kings. For instance, the King of Jericho was a vassal of Solomon, the King of Jerusalem. And the King of Jerusalem was himself a vassal of *Ha'Shem,* the *Melekh malkhey ha'm'lokhim ha'kadosh barukh hu.*

When the Shah ruled Iran, he was called the *shahanshah,* the King of Kings. That is the way they had it, and it goes back to the Hittite emperor who was *sharru rabbu,* the absolute monarch of many vassal kingdoms.

So when we use the phrase *Ribbono shel Olam, Ha'Shem Melekh,* we are speaking about an ultimate King of Kings. In *hasidus,* in *kabbalah,* it is explained that there can't be a king without subjects. So who makes God a King? *We do. Keter Yitnu l'kha,* " We offer You the crown," we surrender to Your will. *We do that.* That is a contribution we make.

But many people have become disenchanted with the metaphor of the King. So if you no longer accept a governing hierarchy, what do you deal with in relation with God? You deal with an organism. In the past, the Rabbis put it this way: "Just the soul fills and invigorates the body, the Holy One, blessed be He, fills and invigorates the universe."

This *organismic* view of the world is what I want to get back to so that we can understand our interaction with God. There are some people who want an abstract monism, but alas, it doesn't exist. People who want an organismic monism have more to work with. For we are all cells of the greater being. Every cell, every part of the body contributes something to the whole, and also receives something from the whole. We are all connected in a kind of *share-flow* that goes from organ to organ, and from limb to limb.

In energy healing, there is a remarkable process called the Body Talk System. Instead of trying to diagnose what is wrong with you, I ask your body. The discoverers of this process first began with kinesiology, and now they querying the body directly. They point out that one of the reasons illness happens in the body is because organs don't talk to each other. Sometimes a gland will not get the right message from another. Sometimes an inner organ won't get the right message from another one. So what do they do? They ask the body, "In which order should we begin to connect the various inner parts?" And in this way the person gets to a greater level of health. With the body of the world in its current state of illness, I wonder if we could apply a similar process.

Recently, I talked to a friend of mine who was at the Parliament of Religions. As usually happens in these great meetings, everyone says nice things, speaking from the *ought* of their tradition, but nothing much happens from it. What would have happened if all these people who were at the Parliament of Religions would have been able to say, "We are cells of the greater planetary organism, and we have to work together so that there should be a *share-flow* between us"?

Tikkun Olam, the rectification of our world, is brought about by the deposits we make into the shared pool of *K'nesset Yisrael,* which is the *Shekhinah.* When the *Shekhinah* is honored in the right way, we call this giving power to the *pamalya shel'ma'ala,* to the heavenly 'family.' It is like saying: *Gadlu l'Adonai ittiy un'rommamu sh'mo yakhdav,* let's come together to enlarge and charge-up the God-field. *Yitgadal v'yitkadash sh'may rabbah.* We are saying, "Magnify, sanctify, put in more, put in more."

When we come to *shul,* there is a *pushke,* a charity box, into which we deposit a little money before we pray. In the same way, we might ask, "How many ergs did I put into *Klal Yisrael* with my *davvenen* today; how much did I contribute to the healing of the planet?"

Kavvanah

There is a discussion in the Talmud that says: *Mitzvot tz'rikhot kavvanah,* "Does a *mitzvah* need to have intentionality behind it or not?"* For instance, when you're baking *matzah,* you roll the dough out and you say: *L'shem matzot mitzvah.* Unless you state your intention (*kavvanah*) that that this dough should be used to make *matzot* for Pesah, in order to fulfill the commandment, the *matzot* are lacking something.

What is "lacking" has nothing to do with the physical wholeness. If we are only dealing with physical matter, the *matzah* without *kavvanah* would still be physically complete, it is just that it would be psychically void of that which it needs to be spiritually complete for the sake of the *mitzvah.* Likewise, a bill of divorce needs to be written *Lishmo, Lishmah u'l'shem gerushin.* That is to say, the scribe has to state explicitly that he is writing the bill of divorce for a specific man and woman in order to make it a potent instrument for effecting the divorce. If it lacks the intention, even if it is letter perfect, the mechanical work is invalid and powerless to affect its purpose.

Thus, *T'fillah bli kavvanah k'guf bli n'shamah,* "Prayer without *kavvanah* is like a body without a soul."* So *kavvanah* is what energizes prayer and makes it alive. Of all the *kavvanot,* the most essential *kavvanah,* the ground in which all the other *kavvanot* are grounded is called *Kabbalat ol malkhut Shamayim.* It is real when we can say, "I accept upon myself the yoke of God's kingdom." The current meaning of this is this: *I accept that I am an integral part of the whole and don't wish to act like a 'rogue cell,' a cancer cell in the greater body. I want to collaborate with all of life, and be in harmony with the will of the Creator.*

This is the most basic *kavvanah.*

---

* Talmud, B'rakhot 13a.

* Bahyah ibn Pakuda (11th century), Spanish Jewish rabbi and philosopher.

When someone is about to convert to Judaism, we ask them to state clearly that they accept upon themselves the yoke of God's kingdom, dip in the *mikveh* once, and recite the *Sh'ma'*. All this is like saying, "From now on, God is my boss." Then we ask them to state clearly that they accept the yoke of the divine commandments and dip again.

Suppose I were to ask even the most religiously observant person, someone who was totally transparent, open and willing to talk frankly, about how well he is doing with *lashon ha'ra'*, with talking gossip behind a person's back. I might compare his answer with how very careful he is about the laws of the Sabbath. We might see that, for all his commitment to bearing the yoke of the divine commandments, he is somehow deficient when it comes to *lashon ha'ra'*.

We are not perfect; everyone has a flaw. Everyone has something that they could do better. For instance, when it comes to respecting nature—*Oy!* We earthlings have been deficient for a long time. Look at the way it was in the time of Ruth. She goes out while the people are harvesting their wheat and picks up wheat from the corner of the field that the poor are entitled to take as their due of the harvest of agriculture. It was their due.

The rules were very clear. They had to be careful about what you could plant together and what you couldn't, and to protect the quality of the soil. All these rules were very real for us at one time. Then came the exile, and we lost our connection with the Earth. These days, we have to start learning from indigenous people to find out what the Earth wants to tell us.

To use a metaphor for *kavvanot* from the world of computers: What instructions do I have on my system files for consciousness that I would like to live by? If I could get to these instructions, I might read: (a) that I am doing this for God's sake; (b) that I am integral to the universe; or (c) that I want to live in such a way that I should

should be totally in harmony with existence. If I say ,
"God with the Torah created the world, then the world is
like the Torah—sometimes we get Torah from the world,
and sometimes we the get the world from the Torah. It
goes back and forth as any organic system flows back
and forth. The *kavvanah* has to be the subtext.

Imagine I am saying some prayers:

Here are the words that I am saying;
Here is the translation of what I am saying,
Here is the deeper level of meaning,
Here is the loving and devotional meaning;
Here is the mystical meaning.

You see how the levels are stacked one on top of the
other? In my book, *Paradigm Shift*, I did the symphonic
score for the first blessing of the *Amidah* to show: What
do we do with the body? What do we do with the mind?
It's not simple. We have all these all these layers, and
they are active in us at the same time. *Kavvanah* is the
ability to keep steering our consciousness while being
aware of all those layers.

Imagine I am in the cockpit of an airplane, revving up
the engines and checking all of the gauges. Before I take
off, I want to know if all my gauges are on. Am I getting
the right feedback? That is also the way in which we use
our *kavvanot*. We ask ourselves, "Is my body ready?"
Then we do the *Birkhot Ha'Shahar*. "Is my heart ready?"
Then we do the *P'sukei d'Zimrah*. "Is my mind ready?"
Then we do the *Kriyat Sh'ma'* and its blessings. Finally we
come to the *Amidah*. So that is the way in which we attune, bringing all these things together.

But there are some things that we don't want to ask
with a lot of *kavvanah*. According to the kabbalists, the
hand with its five fingers is like a *Heh*, whose numerical
equivalent is five. A coin in that hand is like a point, the
Yud. An arm reaching-out is like a *Vav*. And the hand re-
cieving the coin is another *Heh*. Thus, when you give

tzedakah, charity, they say you create the unification of the divine name, *Y-H-V-H*.

Whenever you do a *mitzvah* you are supposed to make a *b'rakhah*—you have to say a blessing. Thus we thank God for commanding us to put on *t'fillin*, for commanding us to put on the *tallit*, to wave the *lulav* and *etrog*. So the question is—Why don't we say a blessing before giving *tzedakah*? The answer is, never mind your *kavvanah*; here you actually need to *do* good for someone else. Could you imagine if someone said, "I want to give you *tzedakah*, and I know you are very hungry, but I need to go to the *mikveh*, put on my *tallit* and *t'fillin*, so I can say the blessing with great *kavvanah*." In the meantime, the poor guy dies from hunger.

You see, it is imperative. *Et La'assot La'Ha'Shem heferu toratekha*. There is a time to do something for God and you must let go of the Torah and your concern about your own spirituality. At this point, your giving *tzedakah* is more important. Therefore, there is *kavvanah* in this element too that says, "I'm throwing the *kavvanah* out, because my only intention at this point is that this person will not be hungry, that she will get what she needs."

Now, there is another level of *kavvanah*, and that is to send merit. Sometimes you give some *tzedakah* because you want healing for someone else. We often make a *misheberakh* in *shul* for someone to be healed. Then we give *tzedakah*, and the *kavvanah* is that the *tzedakah* should affect the healing. We have that from our funeral tradition, where people would go around with *pushkes* and say that *tzedakah* saves you from death. The notion is that this is the way you give back to the world.

I might have a *kavvanah*—"Why am I giving this *tzedakah*? Because I would like a certain result." Is it kosher to do that? Yes and No!

Sometimes the Rabbis of the Talmud say that if you give *tzedakah* with the expressed intention that your child should be healed, this is not the best motivation. But I think this is a wonderful motivation; for the one who offers *tzedakah* in this way takes for granted that God is real for us, saying: "This is what I need from You, *Ha'Shem*."

In recent years, there has been much talk of *The Secret*, and the secret was *affinity*, the universe affirming what you think and what you want. Here you have a power, a *kavvanah*.

Imagine that *kavvanah* is dealing with the healing of the planet. If enough people were to make a shared 'battery' for that healing, putting all our *kavvanah* together, just think what we could achieve.

I want to invite us all to make our *kavvanah* available for that healing; and if there is someone who needs a healing or help from heaven, my *kavvanah* should be available to them when they need it. And let us say *Amen*.

Question and Answer Session

Comment: I have a habit, developed over many years, of davvening everything given in the *siddur*. I found it very difficult—even after learning in the *Keter Shem Tov*[*]—to attach myself to the word and elevate it with myself in the middle of the prayers; it stops you from proceeding down the line of the page. I asked permission, then I said, "Is that okay?" And now I hear you saying again that it's okay.

Reb Zalman: Let me put it to you this way: imagine you have to talk to me about something, and you have a whole speech written out. You come with your speech and I say: "Chaskale, I love you. Put this piece of paper down. What is really on your mind?" If God is real to a

---

[*] An anthology of teaching by the Ba'al Shem Tov edited by Rabbi Ahron ben Tzvi HaKohen of Apt.

person, then the other thing falls away: *Just tell me where you are, what's real for you.*

But if you make 'public policy' that says, "There are no standards, and everything goes," then this is no good either. So you have to *entrain* a person, as we were, to *davven* the whole thing. Indeed, there are days when there is nothing else that we need or can do. We need to do it that way then. But often, when the moment of grace comes along, and God says: "Never mind; I have a goody to give to you," you say, "Sorry, I have to *davven.*" This is how some people do the *Haggadah:* "Daddy, daddy — why do we eat *matzah?*" "Shut up and read the *Haggadah.*" The whole purpose is *v'higgad'ta l'vinkha.* When your child asks you a genuine question, and you miss the opportunity because of rigid adherence to form, it's such a pity.

Comment: I just love what you're saying, because a lot of times when I'm davvening, if I have to say everything, it just kills it for me. I just sit there, and the more I read it, the more I find that I'm not participating, not really finding what I'm looking for.

Reb Zalman: Well, I want to say something about how I feel that we are not doing it right. The pews and the chairs are a problem, because we sit down in them and become like a piece of furniture ourselves.

Imagine if people would stand closely around the *Ba'al T'fillah,* and as he or she begins, they would all raise their voices slightly; it would really take off. It would be so much different. Then I don't think you would necessarily need to go your own way, because you'd be caught up in the rhythm of the communal prayer. Sometimes Reb Marc begins with a rhythmic thing that everyone joins and it's wonderful.* At that point, you don't even

---

* Rabbi Marc Soloway, spiritual leader of Congregation Bonai Shalom in Boulder, Colorado.

want to say: "I don't have anything to do with that be-cause I'm doing my own thing." You are already *caught* by it; you are drawn into it.

But let's say the prayer leader says *Ashrei* fast and then reads the last sentence out loud, and in-between nothing is happening, and there is a lot of dead space. Well, you can race along from one end to the other, or you can say "No! I'm going to do it differently and find myself in this *davvenen.*"

Myself, I like the sentence, *Poteah et yadekha u'massbiya l'khol hay ratzon,* "You open up your hand and you satisfy every living being with what they need." So I might stick with that sentence for a while, for *Karov Ha'Shem l'khol kor'av,* God is close to those who call out in truth. Often, staying with some aspect of the prayer is so much more satisfying than rushing after the *shaliah tzibur.*

Comment: There's a challenge that comes sometime in the *matbe'ah t'fillah.* Sometimes I'll see something and it challenges me to think about it and ask myself, "What is my consciousness about that?" I have conversations with *Ha'Shem* about things that maybe I wouldn't think to converse with Him otherwise, especially in the parts of the *Amidah* about the judges of old. I start to talk to *Ha'Shem* and say: "You know, maybe we should be care-ful how we pray to You. Maybe You're giving us what we pray for even though they're not so good. Why are we doing this?" Or, "Maybe You took this away from us because You are trying to tell us that a different para-digm would be better. Maybe You're not punishing us." I question pieces of history and pieces of my impression of history. Sometimes even in the course of that *t'fillah.*

In this way, the meaning of the prayers has changed over time for me as I've had different experiences. Sud-denly I'll say, "Ah, that really speaks to me now," whereas in another time it didn't. So there's a benefit for me in allowing myself the freedom in prayer to sit under the *tallit* and have a conversation, and a benefit from go-

ing through the whole *t'fillah* as well. It helps me to figure out where I am on the traditional/non-traditional
issues.

Reb Zalman: It depends a lot on what you have been
paying attention to. I'll give you an example:

An issue is coming up at the Supreme Court.
Ha'shivah shofteynu, "bring back justice." I say these
words, but the words for me are like an *aide de memoire* —
Don't forget to pray about justice! That's what this one
means. Don't forget to pray about the ecology and the
economy in the *Barekh Aleynu*. Don't forget to pray about
all the people who are doing good work in the world.

That is what I call 'illustrative,' not 'normative.' I
think it is important to recognize that a lot of Torah is illustrative and not normative. There are some people who
claim that it is always normative. But this notion doesn't
work anymore. This is one of the reasons why I am talking about davvenology, because I want to help people in
their relationship with God.

Comment: I find myself in the opposite situation. I go to
the extreme of only doing *hitbodedut,* of only doing it for
my heart. I almost never do structure *(keva)*, and sometimes I miss it. I've conditioned myself to throw it away,
and I struggle with that.

Reb Zalman: An athlete, a somatatone, will *davven* differently than an emotional viscerotone. A cerebrotonic person will be happy just to contemplate *ehad* for an hour.*
So there are the individual differences from the beginning. Likewise, some people are more 'right-brain.' And
some more 'left-brain.' A left-brainer will want to say
everything as it is in the book. The right-brainer will
want to daydream more, to have more enchantment with

---

* Using psychologist, Dr. William Sheldon's typology, also used by Aldous
Huxley in his writings.

God. I want to tell you, the saddest thing today is that there is so little enchantment.

When I was in Cracow, I walked into the *shul* of the ReMA' — Rabbi Moshe Isserles, who added the Ashkenazic glosses to the *Shulhan Arukh* — and I had the sense of needing to tiptoe. It is not like entering a big synagogue today, with all the plaques of people who have donated to it, a modern *bar-mitzvah* factory and lifecycle celebration facility, where nothing else is happening. But when you come into a place like the *shul* of the ReMA', so filled with holy awe, you begin to feel: "Oh, the ReMA' is here. The Megalleh Amukot — the great kabbalist, Rabbi Natan Nata Shapiro — is here." These are the people who davvened in that place, and their vibration is still around. So that has to do with enchantment.

When people would go out on Friday afternoon and say, *Lekha dodi lekrat kallah*, let's go outside, into the fields to greet the Shabbat Queen, that is enchantment. *Nebbukh,* it is much easier to have enchantment in the hills of Judea. There is a hotel in those hills where we once had a wonderful week of study. You can see *Shabbat* is coming. You can almost see from there to the Mediterranean, into which the sun descends, and you can smell the field there. You live in a fairytale, as it were.

If you can't go into the fairytale, at least once a week, your life is going to be too dry.

We also need to ask ourselves, "To what am I best attuned?" There is some music that will make me want to get deeper into *Shabbat*. I once made a recording called, *Prelude for a Rendezvous with the Beloved: Kabbalat Shabbat*. That is my *Shabbat* audio *mikveh*. I hear that, and it just takes me to the place I need to be.

This also has to do with enchantment. Wherever things have gotten too prosaic, you need a little enchantment. It is the difference between *Misnagdishe* Judaism and *Hasidishe* Judaism. More than anything we need enchantment today.

Today, hardly any Jew is a Jew because they can't help it. We are more and more *Jews by choice.* We are all using our choices, and knowing that helps us to say: "What can I give You, *Ribbono shel Olam? I choose* You."

Comment: I grew up with a Conservative Jewish education, and ten years ago, I got into Buddhist meditation practice and have been practicing it regularly ever since. I started to notice, little by little, that the majority of my meditation teachers were Jewish. When we talk about being "Jewish by choice," I understand that on the level of being implicitly and externally Jewish and having Jewish practices, but I never really considered myself someone who really had a 'prayer practice' (at least not in a conventional sense). Now I have started to realize that I do. I acknowledge that I do. And now I'm starting to fill in the pieces, bringing more of the *siddur* back in and incorporating it into my practice.

Reb Zalman: It has to do with grounding. Jack Kornfield says, *"After the Ecstasy, the Laundry."* I look at all the Jewish Buddhists, like Jack Kornfield and Sylvia Boorstein, and I see that they have really grounded things. They are not so much interested in the abstract, but to say, "Now let's go. Where are we?" That also exists in Zen Buddhism, in the Rinzai school of Zen. It says, "Don't go all high falutin; just do it."

When the Dalai Lama says that what is most important is that we should have a secular ethic, he means something empirical. *Karma,* in a way, is a "secular ethic." It doesn't say that God is going to punish you. It says that what you are doing causes particular situations.

But when it comes to that kind of understanding, I look at Bernie Glassman Roshi. Here is a Jew who was made a Zen lineage holder by his teacher. Then he realized that that was not exactly what he wanted to do and he turned this role over to someone else. Then he started to make "street retreats," homeless retreats, and started to hold retreats in Auschwitz. Why? I think this is in our nature. When I look at Rahm Emanuel at the right hand of the President, doing what he can for *Tikkun Olam;* When I look at Ben Bernanke, who has all the keys to the economy in his hand, trying to steer right, there is a certain pride I take in our genetic endowment to want to heal and ground things.

Can you imagine what would have happened in the Catholic Church if St. Teresa of Avila and St. John of the Cross—who were both of Jewish *converso* familes—would have married and had children? But instead, the Church culled the best people and took them out of the genetic pool by making sure that they should be celibate. But in the Jewish system, a rich man who had a daughter, would go to the *yeshivah* to find the right kind of groom for his daughter, so that there should be *Torah u'g'dullah b'makom ehad,* learning and influence in same family. That went on for generations and generations and generations, and became a nice thing for Jewish society, even when Torah observance fell off among some generations.

If you look at the 1930s and see who were the social organizers of the unions, you will find many Jews. Long ago, peope used to talk about, "red diaper babies," whose parents were socialists. Though they were secular, they truly believed that they could make the world better place.

I'll tell you a funny story. In Winnipeg, where I used to live, there was the provincial Parliament. The provincial parliament has districts, and every district has a representative. In Winnipeg, there was a district called the "Lower North End." That was where the Jews, Ukrainians, Russians, and Poles lived. And there was a guy who lived there named Moshe Gray. His real name was Guraryeh, but he went by Gray, and he was a member of the Parliament.

Well, Moshe Gray and a buddy would go to the *shvitz* on *Shabbat* mornings, and when we had finished *davve-*

nen, he would come to make *Kiddush* with us in the Lubavitcher *shul*. That was his is way of doing *Shabbat!*

Anyway, Moshe Gray called me one day and said: "You know, every year I give a talk in Parliament, and it is printed out in the Parliament journal; it enters the public record. I've been saying for years that I am a socialist—not a socialist from Marx, but a socialist from Isaiah." Then he said, "But I'm tired already of being a socialist only from Isaiah. Could you help me to be a socialist from Jeremiah maybe?" By the time he died, years later, we he had already become a socialist from *Pirkei Avot!*

So there is something wonderful that filters through, that says, "I want to make life easier for people; I want to make it more secure; I want people to have food and shelter." So may we all have security and food and shelter and *v'nomar — Amen!*

Sixth Talk

Blue Jeans Spirituality

Whenever we talk about the Four Worlds of Kabbalah, it sounds like we are going into spiritual places, far away. But it is not really so far away from us. It all has to do with how we are engaging them, here and now. To make this clearer, I once wrote some simple lyrics to a melody that my friend, Reb Shlomo Carlebach composed long ago:

Lord I want to do for you;
Lord I want to feel for you;
Lord I want to know for you;
Lord I want to be for you.

You are action;
You are feeling;
You are knowledge;
You are being.

You are action;
You are feeling;
You are knowledge;
You just are.

This is a way of understanding how we relate to the Four Worlds. When you look at spirituality from that perspective, you get a sense that this is where we are all the time. We are in *action,* and in *feeling,* and in *knowing,* and in *being,* and these are not things that have to do with 'other worlds.' These are all a part of our here and now.

Up to this point, I have talked about *hitbonenut, d'veikut, kavvanah,* and many other wonderful things, but now I want to talk about spirituality in a very simple way.

My friends, the brothers Nathan and Joseph Segal, once wrote a simple tune for a recording of the Reb Nahman's *Tale of the Seven Beggars:*

> *Rabbi Nahman of Bratzlav used to say,*
> *Friends, do not despair,*
> *For difficult time is come upon us,*
> *Joy must fill the air.*

It is a "difficult time" now, and all of these wonderful things I have discussed, need to be used on a daily basis. It is easy to do them when you are on retreat, or participating in a celebration, but don't think that they are not applicable to everyday issues and problems. Most of the time when we talk about *davvenen* and spirituality, we distance ourselves from everyday problems. But that is where we need all this the most, in the everyday. How do you stay 'spiritual' when you are shopping, or when you are doing the dishes, or when you are taking the kids to school? Unless we install spirituality into our ordinary lives, it won't help us much.

There is a wonderful line in the daily *davvenen* that says: *U'k'doshim b'khol yom y'hal'lukha selah,* 'the holy ones praise you everyday.' But I read it as, "Those who are holy in the everyday, praise You." The real praise for God is not the holiness that people have in their holy places, but in the everyday.

Take a look at how basic that is to Jewish life. We have *tzitzit,* the fringed garment, and it says that they will "remind you" of what it is all about.* We wear the *t'fillin* in the morning to remind us of what it is all about. At the door, we have a *mezuzzah* to remind us that we are going from one realm into another realm. It says, "Stay awake, stay aware; don't space out." These are everyday re-

---

minders which the Torah gives us, and this is how the the everyday routines can really make for *u'k'doshim b'khol yom,* for everyday holiness.

So what happens? Most of the time we have that pang of conscience — "You should do better!" When does it come? Usually after we have done something wrong. We say, "Oops!" after we have made a mistake. If we could possibly have the technology to say, "Oops!" *before* we make the mistake, that would be wonderful. This is what I was talking about when I mentioned 'memory resident programs,' just like a virus detector. Once the virus attempts to enter the system, an alarm sounds and the virus is quarantined. It is good that the alarm sounds before rather than after, because if it came after, we would have a lot of trouble.

If we could create such a situation in our moral life, that would be wonderful. This is why I think 'reminders' like the *t'fillin, tzitzit,* and the *mezuzzah* are so important. Nowadays we do these things in *shul.* We put on the *t'fillin* and *tallit* in *shul.* But they don't help us very much when we are not in *shul.* The only thing that helps us is the *mezuzah,* because we have that to remind us of our moral awareness when we go through the door.

On my car, I have painted the letter *shin* with the three prongs on the right side of the car and a *shin* with four prongs on the left side of the car. It is this way because, on the *t'fillin,* there is a *shin* with three prongs on the right side of the *t'fillin* box, and one with four prongs on the left side. So this is another way of saying, "I want to bring those reminders into more of my everyday life."

The *mezuzzah* on my office door has a button that I can press, so that when pass through the door, I hear, "Wake up as you cross this threshold." This is wonderful, because that is what a *mezuzzah* is supposed to do.

We have ritual routines that we do, but most of them we do as if asleep and we don't wake up enough for them.

In the middle of the morning *davvenen*, I have the *t'fillin* on, and I touch the *t'fillin* on my arm and my head — as prescribed by the tradition at certain points in the liturgy — and bring my fingers to my lips, and may not be aware what I am doing, because it has become routine. If I were to just stop for a moment and ask myself, "What am I about to do?" I might answer, "I'm about to dedicate my heart and my arm and my head to the service of God." I have to make explicit what is implicit in all these things.

Living in the Everyday Presence of God

So how do I go about doing my everyday spirituality? It's a pity that we have to have an alarm clock today. I wish that we could have a much gentler way of waking into the day. The alarm rings and the heart pumps adrenaline into the blood. Thus, the entry into our day is as if we are a danger. The word 'alarm' points to that. We rush through getting dressed, and try to get everything else done faster. We eat breakfast quickly, make sure to have hi-test coffee, get into the car, braving traffic, and arriving at our workplace completely frazzled.

We really need something more like the Zen alarm clocks which chime so gently and sweetly.

When I was in Bombay in 1982 for the Transpersonal Psychology Conference, I woke up every morning and went down to the boardwalk for a walk. There I found Bombay's finest gentlemen and ladies taking their morning constitutional at the side of the bay, walking at a restful, savoring pace, all before turning to their daily work.

Mahatma Gandhi had a student Vinobha Bhave, who was imprisoned together with other Indians in a British camp in India. Every morning, a raucous bell would wake the prisoners, and there was often rioting. Bhave went to the prison authorities and told them that he has a way to reduce the amount of rioting, and asked them not to use those bells. They refused. So he asked them for permission to get up earlier, which they granted. About 20 minutes before the bell rang each morining, he walked from bunk to bunk, and took the hand of the sleeping people in a gentle way. Then they opened their eyes and greeted him with a smile and the rioting abated.

I like to program a clock for waking Jews. It would begin humming the melody for *Modeh Ani*, rising slowly in volume, and then begin to recite the words of thanksgiving for a good night's sleep, and for the joy of waking into the day. Then I would be able to open my eyes and say: "Oh, how wonderful! Another day. Thank You, God, for giving me another day." That would be an effective beginning of the day.

Then I would tell myself, "Don't forget this in the middle of the day. I want you to stop what you are doing several times today and make a connection. 'Log-on' to this grateful frame of mind again, and be connected through the 'inner-net' to God." At that morning moment, you can make an *act of will* that will work for you during the day to offer an 'arrow prayer.'

In this way, I arm my will by affirming my desire to remember to 'long-on' to this mentality in the middle of my day. I set it up early in the morning so I will be able to tune-in to it during the day, into *shiviti* and to *d'veikut*.

Let me spell this out. I like to say (as I've said before), "This call is being monitored for quality purposes." In other words, there is an awareness that I'm not just doing it for you; I would like it to be in the service of God. I'd like to welcome God-awareness and presence into what I'm doing at this time. That has to do with the words, *shiviti Ha'Shem l'negdi tamid*, 'I have set the LORD before me always.'

Now, if you look at the letters of the divine name, *Yud-Heh-Vav-Heh*, you see that the *Yud* is like the head, the *Heh* like the shoulders and arms, the *Vav* like the torso, the other *Heh* like the pelvis and the legs. This is another way of saying that I'm not so far from God, because I know that Y-H-V-H is inside of me, already present there. I don't have to go far to find this. As it says in *Torah: Ki karov eleakha ha'davar m'od b'fikha uvil'vav'kha la'assoto,* 'The thing is so close to you, in your mouth and in your heart that you can do it.'* You don't have to wonder who is going to cross the sea and bring it to you, who is going to climb to heaven and bring it down; it is right here. So when I speak of it as embedded and enfleshed in me, I can say *Miv'sari ehzeh Eloka,* 'From my very flesh do I see God,' and I know that I am made in the silhouette of God.**

When I can say, "This is occurring in the presence of God," that is the first part. The second part is to realize that I can't do it all myself. In order to do it right, in order to do it with full energy, I can't do it by myself. I have to be 'plugged-in' to God, and that's what we call *d'veikut,* 'cleaving,' 'being together.' So I want to say, *Ribonno shel Olam, ha'noteyn lya'ef ko'akh,* "You are the One who gives energy to someone who is tired."*** I'm opening myself so that the flow of energy should come in to me, allowing me to do what I have to do. And I don't have to do it with my energy alone; and that's important, because it's not about me. I am deployed to do a task, and if I allow for the One who deploys me, whose agent I am, then I'm not the cause; I'm only the agency through which it happens. That's called *d'veikut.*

How would you do that in a modern way? I don't know what you use for your screensaver, but each one of my computers scrolls a sentence as the screensaver that is reminds me, "We don't know how we will serve our God until we get there."**** Or, "I have set the LORD before me always." On my cell phone, I have a ring tone that sounds the *shofar. Matzah* is not only something that I

---

* Deuteronomy 30:14.

** Job 19:26.

*** *Birkhot Ha'Shahar,* in the morning prayers.

**** Exodus 10:26.

want to remember on Passover; I have a *shmurah matzah,* a hand-baked *matzah,* in a plastic bag hanging in my meditation room together with an old *lulav* and *etrog.* They say to me: "Don't forget freedom. Don't forget the ecology." These reminders ground us as the world tries to pull us in too many directions.

When we begin with a general *kavvanah* in the morning, saying, "Whatever I do today, I want to help me fulfill my purpose in life, the reason for which I was deployed here."

Sometimes people think of *mitzvot* as 'commandments,' like I am being 'bossed around' by someone. In Germany, when Martin Buber and Franz Rosenzweig had their *Lehrhaus,* or *beit ha'midrash* in Frankfurt, they discussed the *mitzvot.* One of them said that *mitzvot* are *Gesetz,* 'legislation,' the law. The other one said that *mitzvah*s are *Gebot,* 'commandments,' someone has commanded you and you have to fulfill it. Then there was a Rabbi Leo Baeck . . .*

Rabbi Leo Baeck once caused me some embarrassment. I used to be the rabbi of an Orthodox *shul* in New Bedford, Massachusetts. And from time to time, two colleagues (one a Conservative rabbi and the other a Reform rabbi) and I would hold "trialogues." The three of us used to go around presenting our version of Judaism, and you can imagine how each of us wanted to look like the best. At that time, I said: "Religion is in the business of making saints. In Orthodoxy" — I was very much a card-carrying Orthodox Hasidic rabbi then — "we have saints. Where are your saints?" I would ask. The Conservative rabbi couldn't say anything. This was before Abraham Joshua Heschel marched with Martin Luther King Jr. But the Reform rabbi shot back, "What about Leo Baeck?" I couldn't respond, because Leo Baeck was the great and compassionate Reform rabbi of the German

---

* Rabbi Leo Baeck (1873-1956) was a German-Jewish scholar and important Jewish leader during the Holocaust.

concentration camp, Theresienstadt. He was the one who kept up the morale of people there. He was a saint.

Now Baeck said the *mitzvah* is not a commandment, not a law, but as a secret, a *Geheimniss;* a *mitzvah* is a secret shared between the soul and God.

Let me illustrate this:

Imagine I at a gathering, and my wife Eve is on the other side of the room. I unobtrusively send her a glance and a gesture of love as if to say, *I'm talking to all these people here, but I want you to know that I love you,* and she responds with a wink, *I love you too.* This is how it is when I fulfill a *mitzvah;* I am sending a secret message to God. This is what you can do in the middle of the day. I can do it right now: *I am winking at You,* Ribbono shel Olam; *I hope you like what I am doing.*

If I were a waiter in a restaurant, I would want to serve the food with a wink that says, *God! Let them enjoy the food and eat in good health.*

These are tiny moments of awareness called 'arrow prayers,' meaning that you shoot them off like arrows. You don't linger for a long time with them; you just send them off.

Our father Jacob said, "This is how I dealt with it, with my sword and with my bow."* The traditional translation is, "With my prayer and with my pleading and my worship." In other words, what is the sword that he used? It was his ability to pray and worship.

Reb Ahrele Roth took up the idea of Bahyah ibn Pakuda who wrote the classic, *Duties of the Heart.* We have 613 commandments, or duties. Many are done with action, but few are done with speech. Rabbinic commandments have a lot to do with speech, but scriptural commandments don't. But some commandments have to do with awareness: "You shall know it today and set it on

---

* Genesis 48:22.

your heart: that the *Y-H-V-H* is God, in the heavens above and the earth below; nothing else exists."* This is a commandment of awareness.

There are thirty-two commandments of awareness gathered by Reb Ahrele Roth.

I used to have a lot of little brass bells from India, and would give them to people to use them in their car, as I did; for every time I hit a pothole or a bump, it would ring, and remind me to send up an arrow prayer, which had to do with awareness. I trained myself to do that because, once I had a notion that if, God forbid, I would get into an automobile accident, I would want to 'go' with one of those sacred thoughts instead of the deprecation of the accident.

Most of the time when people are involved in things having do with Jewish prayer, they think of the *siddur*, because there is a lot written about how to do the prayers in the *siddur*. That's good. But very few people ask the question: "How did the *siddur* ever come about?"

If I go to Psalm 34, I find that King David was in trouble, having fallen into the hands of Philistines. He had to run away from King Saul, who was trying to kill him, and was caught by the Philistines who also had a price on his head. So they brought David to the king of the Philistines who was going to kill him.

The Midrash tells a nice story. King David wanted to find out what's the use of a spider, and what's the use of crazy people. So once when he was running away from King Saul and hiding in a cave, a spider wove a web over the entrance. King Saul, coming to the entrance to that part of the cave, figured that there was no use in looking there because the spider web was not torn. But later David is brought to the king of the Philistines, and he begins to act crazy, foaming at the mouth. The king says, "Do I need more crazy people around me?" So they

---

* Deuteronomy 4:39.

threw him out, and this is how King David's life was saved.

Psalm 34 has an acrostic in it which describes that this is the song that King David made after he had pretended to be a crazy man and the king of the Philistines sent him away. And when he was on his way home, he gave thanks.

What do you do when you want to remember a poem without being able to write it down at the moment? You do it with the alphabet: (a) you're adorable; (b) you're beautiful . . . There are other compositions in the Bible, especially in the Psalms, that are arranged in alphabetical order. Later on, this too was the way in which other compositions and liturgy were arranged—according to alphabetical order, or acrostics of the name of the author, or the occasion.

So David comes back to where his friends are camped; he is exhausted, hungry, and thirsty, and his friends welcome him to the campfire. I see the camp almost like in a Western movie where they are cooking beans over a fire. He says, "Have you got some grub for me?" They serve him, and after eating, he leans back and gets mellow. His friends, knowing that he is about to sing, bring him a lyre, the equivalent of a guitar. He begins to strum the instrument, and then sings them that song which became Psalm 34.

Now this song was written down much later in ancient paleo-Hebrew letters and then transliterated into the Hebrew letters that were used after the return from Babylon. Eventually it got into the Bible and was printed, and now we have the words, but *only* the words. There are so many dimensions to the psalm, dimensions that have to do with David's inner experience. In the biblical text, there are no vowels and no cantillation marks, no clear sentence dividers. Where is the sentiment that was in that psalm? It was composed spontaneously by David in gratitude, "Oh, my life was saved!" So allow yourself to imagine this until you can almost feel it.

I call these prayers (especially those found in the prayer book) 'freeze-dried prayers,' like freeze-dried soup. That is to say, they have the main ingredients, but lack that which will reconstitute them to their original fullness. If I give you freeze-dried soup to eat with a spoon and I don't add the water, it wouldn't have any *ta'am*; it would be tasteless.

Most people get the *siddur* and expect it to live for them, when really it is like a freeze-dried experience; you have to add the water of your own *kavvanah* to bring it to life.

After a while, the Jewish tradition had acquired many prayers and poems, and the Rabbis eventually put them into different orders (prayer rites) and made them mandatory, saying, "This is what you need to recite." Maimonides tells us that the commandment that we should pray has two forms: the rabbinic and the scriptural. The rabbinic form is that in the morning, the afternoon, and the evening you say the prescribed prayers. And before you go to sleep, you say another prayer. All these prayers are set out according to the rabbinic rule.

The scriptural rule about prayer is this: If you need something, talk to God about it. When you feel that you need to speak to God, or ask something from God, you have fulfilled the weightier requirement of prayer. Reb Shalom Dovber of Lubavitch, the father of my *rebbe*, told his disciples, "I will show you how you can take the rabbinic command and turn it in the scriptural commandment." So they asked, "How?" He replied, "If you mean it." That is to say, if you recite words of the rabbinic liturgy with sincereity, as a personal request from you, and you say it *ada'ta d'nafshey*, expressing your own personal prayer, you fulfill both the rabbinic *and* the scriptural command to pray.

This is why I want to say to rabbis — very few people get a chance to pray for what they really need when they come to *shul*. "Go to page" such-and-such and do this and that, and then say the *Kaddish*, and you are finished. You never get the invitation to bring what it is that you really need up to God. Therefore, I've asked people who lead services, when they open up the ark before they take out the Torah, to let people sit for a while, and if they want, to cover themselves with the *tallit* and pray at the open ark for whatever it is they really need.

There is a custom to honor someone in the congregation by opening the ark for them, especially during the high holy days. What is the point of that? The point is: *This is your opportunity to stand before the Torah, and to pour out your heart and offer your prayers!*

Going to Shul

Perhaps you are saying: "Okay, these are the things that I will do at home. When I get up, I will say the *Modeh Ani* and be grateful. Then I will go to the bathroom and wash my hands afterwards, and I will say the blessing: 'Thank you God for giving me a body that works.' Later I will say the blessings over the food before I eat. And after I've eaten, I will *bentsh*, saying the blessing after eating."

So we have home observance intentions.

What is it that you need to do when you go to *shul*? How do you make *shul* count for you? For many people, shuls today have become lifecycle facilities, just for weddings, funerals, bar and bat-mitzvahs. The rest of the time, most people don't even show up. For the people who come to *shul* regularly, what is it that they need to do in order to prepare themselves for *shul*?

I'm grateful that many Jewish Renewal congregations now have vessels for washing your hands before going in to the High Holy Days services. In Europe, that was simply part of the regular routine. The Yemenite Jews not only wash their hands, they also wash their feet as Muslims do, because they come to *shul* barefoot.

This is not generally being done in our synagogues today. I ask myself, "How do I want to enter into the sanctuary?" The *siddur* says the following: "Through Your abundant kindness, I will enter into Your home. I will bow down before You." But we only do this in song; but it needs to be experienced on some level. Have you ever seen a good Catholic coming into church? They come in and dip their fingers in a little font of holy water, and they sprinkle some on themselves or they make the sign of the cross on themselves with the water. Then they come in, and genuflect in the direction of the altar. They bow down. Where did they get that? From us.

In the past, I would sometimes take my students to a church to show them how much the Christian tradition borrowed from us. For instance, before Vatican II, the priest used to wash his hands as part of the Mass before the Sacrament. He would say, "I wash my hands among the innocents." The Hebrew is *Erhatz b'nikayon kappay . . .* "I wash my hands in purity and I circumambulate Your altars, O Lord."

In the Torah, it says that when the *kohen*, the priest is about to go into the sanctuary, he has to wash his hands and his feet. I would like to see people stop before they go in and go through some of this process. I would also like to see the ushers suggesting that people talk outside in the lobby. Once you go in, sit quietly and prepare yourself for prayer. If there would be some nice, quiet music to help people meditate, that would be fine, but don't talk.

I used to do that when I was teaching at the Naropa Institute on Wednesday evenings. I would ask people, "When you come in, please sit quietly for a while and prepare yourself." If I have to interrupt 'social time' and say, "Stop talking," then there is no receptivity. You have to create receptivity.

So we used to say: *Mah tovu ohalekha Ya'akov,* "How good are your tents, O Jacob; your dwelling place, O Israel. Through Your abundant kindness, I will enter Your house and bow down before You." In this way, you get the sense that there is a presence there that is more palpable than on the outside. On the one hand, we say "The whole world is filled with God's glory," but on the other hand, a sanctuary brings this home for us. So I'd like people to walk in on tiptoe. *B'veyt Elohim n'hallekh b'ragesh,* 'into the house of God, we shall enter in a sensitive, feeling way.'

If people don't set their intention before going into *shul,* and do so unconsciously, it is not going to happen for them. What do I want intend before going to *shul?* I'd like to give thanks for the week. I would like to pray for friends and family who are sick, for those who are in mourning, for the ecology of the planet. I want to pray for the president, that with all the pressures, he or she will be able to make good decisions. Whatever intent I set is what I'm going to do when I come to *shul.* Then I want to give thanks saying: *"Oy! Ribonno shel Olam,* it is *Shabbat.* I'm so glad to come to meet You. It was a good week. Some good things happened this week, and I want to thank You for them."

When I walk into a *shul,* I look around and see who is there. In that first look, I want to be able to say, and mean in my heart, "Yes, I love you all." Because it says that before you begin to pray, you should say "I accept upon myself the commandment of loving my neighbor as myself." When I get into that attitude, two things happen: I give up jealousy and judgment.

Imagine I don't like Mr. Stein because he didn't give a big enough donation when he could clearly afford more. Do I want that guy to be able to achieve his total realization? *No.* I don't *fargin* (wish the best for) him. I don't want him to have that. That's how I feel. But it is important to be able to go to *shul* and say, "You and you and you—all of you—may your *davvenen* achieve the highest possibility today; I want the best for you." By saying that, I open it up for myself too. So look around and open yourself to loving as many people as you can see. If you are feeling judgmental about some people, say, "Dear God, whatever judgments I have about this person, please remove them from me, and remove the need to have a judgment about them, so they can live more fully."

There was a great Hasidic master, Reb Pinhas of Koretz, who answered the question: "How can we pray for other people to become better?"* He says that's okay, because we are like holographic parts of each other. I have "you in me and you have the me in you. If I pray for the you in me to be better, then the me in you does something good for you, and then the you in you becomes better." It is organismic to be able to think of other people in a good way: to *fargin* people is the greatest realization.

Now, when you go to *shul*, you have to give yourself permission to 'space-out.' When I come to a beautiful line like, "Everything that breathes praises God," I may not want to go any further than that. It is good enough for now. I may want to play with that for a while, wanting to see "everything that breathes," from elephants down to grasshoppers, each one making a sound, each offering something, breathing in and breathing out. So I give myself permission stay there, and not to go on with everone else. I might just decide to take 'time-out': *I'll catch up with them when they announce the page. Not a problem.*

If you find something significant to you, stay with it. This is the next part of the spiritual work, to be able to say, "This is important to me; this means something to me." Things start lighting up in the mind when we come upon these things, and when that happens, we don't want to rush away from there. We want to savor it because it is a gift we are being given.

---

* Pinhas of Koretz (1726-1791), a disciple of the Ba'al Shem Tov.

Sometimes when I don't feel much like being in my head, I allow myself to go with a melody. There is something that happens when I hear a particular tune, and I go into that dreamy space. I don't need to do much more than that. I can just to let myself float on the sound, even the sound going on in the *shul,* and say: "I'm a child of the universe. I have a right to be here. I'm embraced by the *Shekhinah,* the Divine Presence. Underneath are the everlasting arms. I don't need to do anything; I can just let myself be loved by God in this moment, in this melody." This is another possibility.

But sometimes I also feel like I want to *davven* strongly with everyone else. It's like the song, "Every time I feel that feeling, moving in my heart . . ." Then I move closer and seat myself next to the person leading the prayer. It is like putting a log in the fireplace. If the logs are separated from each other, it's not going to make a good fire. There is something about being in proximity to people who feel fervor in their hearts that turns on on as well. It gives me an attunement, and thus entrains me in that fervor. I want to be close to that.

Maybe when I come into the *shul,* I have something to work out on my own, and so I don't sit in front. I'll sit in the back someplace, in touch with the rest of the *shul,* but not immersed in it. I need to do my own homework at that time, to be with my own inner space.

There is a wonderful psalm that says, "This is a prayer of Moses." I imagine Moses sitting alone during those forty days on the mountain, waiting to be called again to receive revelation. He is looking over his life and he says, "God, You have been our dwelling place from generation to generation."* I translated it this way: "In each incarnation, I was at home with You. Before the worlds, before the mountains were born, You were there. A thousand years in Your sight is like a day gone." Can you imagine, I'm reciting these words in the *siddur,* and I

---

* Psalms 90:1.

decide to put the *siddur* down; I give myself the luxury to go into my imagination, trying to feel how Moses may have felt in saying this.

In my imagination, I can ask myself, "What was Abraham's relationship with God really like?" Or, "What must it have been like when the Ba'al Shem Tov was praying?" These are the kinds of imaginary visits I can make.

Once, I was talking to my son Yotam about a "spiritual Disneyland." If you have been to Disneyland, you know it is a little world unto itself. You go from one place to another, and it is as if you are going from one country to another. And all the while, they are playing a melody, and the melody remains the same, but the overtones have changed, and it now suits the new country. You are in Southeast Asia, then in the Middle East, and it is the same melody. Likewise, I can allow my imagination to take me to Shlomo ibn Gabirol in the Golden Age of Spain, to hear what it was that like when he was praying? Or when Yehuda HaLevi was praying? What must it have been like when Maimonides was saying the word *Ehad*, going into the oneness? These are the kinds of things we can do in *shul* if we want to use our time well.

Imagine the rabbi is about to give a sermon. What would you like to do before the rabbi begins? "Dear God, may the rabbi have something to say that is Your message to me, to help me in my life." This prayer may be a conduit for something significant to reach me. Very often, the rabbi may not even know that he or she is a conduit, but something is going to sneak through because you have already made the channel.

Question and Answer Session

Question: I had a question arise as you were speaking about when you come before God. I wonder — What is that God to you? Who is it that *you* come before? And what is that like?

Reb Zalman: It is a good question.

Once, William James, the psychologist who wrote *Varieties of Religious Experience,* came to a town in New England and asked one of the wardens of a church: "Who is God for you? In front of what do you place yourself in prayer?" The warden said, "An oblong blur." Now he was talking to a New England transcendentalist who was not inclined to think in terms of a form. But while the head may know that there is no form, but the heart needs a root metaphor. I can be in a monist in my head, but I can't be in a monist in my heart. In my heart, I have to have an *other* whom I love. That is where I am in the *I-Thou* relationship.

In the past, people used to think of God as a King. We say *Avinu malkeynu,* 'our Father, our King,' and sometimes we speak of the *Shekhinah* as being our mother, and this is wonderful. But the one that I have the best conversations with is the one who sits in the passenger seat when I'm driving—*my Friend.* I can talk to my friend. I don't have to hide. There is the sense that I am not opaque to God. I don't want to hide anything from God. I can't hide anything from God anyway, but I don't *want* to hide anything from God. I'm transparent, but I also want to talk to God. Part of the divine grace is that God will wear any mask that will allow me to communicate with Him.

H.G. Wells wrote a novel called *The Invisible Man,* which was later made into a movie. But the question was—how were they going to make an invisble man interesting on the screen? Their solution was to wrap him in something; you still wouldn't see his body, but you would see whatever he was wearing, and this gave a visible shape to him. In the same way, we provide God with masks. Sometimes they are terrible and terrifying. But a more motherly God is for me. Then there are some times when I need to have a romance with God. The Sufis are often speaking of God as the Beloved, and sometimes this is precisely how I need to address God. Our own mystics were full of the same imagery. They had a romance with God.

When you say, "Who is it that you come before?" Check out the images that will allow you the most heartful exchange with God. Sometimes, a physical object like a burning candle can be helpful, because it gives you focus.

Question: I wonder if you can say something about God in the present moment. When you were talking about the mind and the heart, and how there has to be a love, a relationship, I began to think of how I can sometimes bring myself to feel present. I am aware of my sensory impressions. I might feel present, but I might not feel connected with my heart, to my feelings. I do feel that there is some way in which the moment is where I find God.

Reb Zalman: What is so wonderful is that we are not composed of only one aspect. If I were to describe my circle of three hundred sixty degrees, there are so many Zalmans in it. Sometimes it is that one that says: "Listen, I don't need to color anything in; I don't need anything fancy. I need to just *be*. Am I right here? Am I right now? Am I in this space and fully here?" And that is enough. Sometimes I want it with a little bit more 'jam' on top. I want to give it a flavor, but I'm not going to say that just because it doesn't have this flavor, or that flavor, that it is wrong.

When a mother is about to give birth and she's experiencing the labor pangs, is it possible for her to say, "I'm with God?" At that point, she really needs to know that she's not alone, that she's not suffering this by herself, that she's working with the flow of life.

When you come to the flow of life, I want to say *L'Hayyim, L'Hayyim.* So much love and many *b'rokhes,* wherever you are going to be in your 'blue jeans.'

Seventh Talk
The Shul and T'shuvah

Into whose domain am I entering when I go to *shul*? Let me go back to a time before we used a building for worship. Native Americans speak of the land as sacred, of holy mountains. When I was in Hawaii, the native peoples often pointed-out sacred places to us. These are the 'chakra points' of the planet, and when you come to them, there is an uncanny feeling that you are moving into someone else's domain, someone else's place. You have entered into a place where there is an invisible, and yet, palpable presence.

In Europe, there used to be shuls like this: you saw the *Ner Tamid* over the *Aron Ha'Kodesh* and you had the sense that you should not engage in loose talk here. Just to make it more clear, there were signs posted that stated that it is forbidden to have any conversation in here. *Assur L'dabber*, you must not speak in *shul* about anything other than prayer.

There was a difference between the sacred domain of a *shul* and the *beit ha'midrash*, the house of study. The *beit ha'midrash* was seen as social space in which you can do what you need to do. People often wanted to eat and sleep there in between their studies. The *beit ha'midrash* didn't have that uncanniness that surrounded some early synagogues and cathedrals before Vatican II. When you walked into one of those cathedrals, you would almost walk on tiptoe, because you'd have a sense that there is a presence facing you. Early in the holy Temple in Jerusalem, you certainly had the sense that, the closer you came to the *Sanctum Sanctorum*, the Holy of Holies, you had to tread very carefully and be almost completely silent.

115

Only the *kohanim*, the priests could go further, because they had to have a greater ritual purity. Then there was the Holy of Holies itself, where only the *kohen gadol*, the high priest was permitted to go, and then only once a year, during Yom Kippur. Can imagine what it must have been like for the *kohen gadol* to enter that space with a golden chain attached to one of his legs, in case he expired there, and they had to pull him out of the space they were not permitted to enter?

You had a real sense of what holy space was about at that time. For us, it is not so clear anymore, especially since a lot of what we have done in Jewish Renewal is in living room congregations. We've gotten people together to sit in a circle, and a different kind of social atmosphere was created. Small groups were also more conducive to ecstatic prayer in the Dionysian mode.

But in a *shul* or a cathedral, the hierarchical Apollonian mode ruled. It was more distant and awe inspiring. In Hasidism, the sentence, "This is my God and I will adore Him, my father's God and I will exalt Him"* is interpreted in this way: "This is my God and I will adore Him" is the Dionysian way, and it is for the *beit midrash;* "My father's God and I will exalt Him" is the Apollonian mode, and this for a *shul.*

So what can you do? It depends what you do at home before you go to *shul.* If you have created a special place inside of yourself, when you come to participate in public worship, you still have that place that you can bring along.

Earlier, I talked about the "lonely place" inside of us. That's the place we go to when we are hurt and sad: "Sometimes I feel like a motherless child" . . . "Nobody knows the troubles I've seen." You are going into that place, and you don't want others to come along. Let me put it in the language of psychology. We regress to more

---

* Exodus 15:2.

primitive levels of awareness of life; we are vulnerable there, and we don't want others to come in and trample and trash our holy place. So you only share that place with very good and intimate friends . . . and with God.

Most people keep that place dark, but you can make a window to let God in. If you go there in the morning, for just a moment, and say, "Dear God, during the day, from time to time, I want to have a few moments with You. Instead of a 'smoke break,' or a 'coffee break,' I want to have a God break, a moment of closness with You. I want to go into that place and just sit quiet for a little while." Then, when you go to *shul*, it is not *their* turf anymore; it belongs to you as well. This is really true, because most of the time, we have a sense that people are expecting something of us.

Not every rabbi is like Reb Tirzah; she will have the expectation that you will come into *shul* with your own God place.* In such a situation, it is not a problem; and more and more in our communities, this is how it goes. But it is not the same everywhere.

The Meditation of Rumination

Now I want to revisit the topic of meditation. For many people, silence and emptying the mind is what meditation is all about. This notion came from the popular introduction of Far Eastern forms of meditation in the 20th century. But that is only one part of the story.

The other day, I heard a story about how some people are afraid that Asian Carp will invade the Great Lakes and spoil the native fish habitat. I have some of the same fears about how Eastern meditation is redefining meditation in other traditions today. But the problem is not Eastern meditation techniques; it is that Jews and Christians haven't maven't made their meditation traditions

---

* Rabbi Tirzah Firestone, founder of the Nevei Kodesh Jewish Renewal Community of Boulder, Colorado.

available to the masses of Jews and Christians. Our own people do not know about meditation in their own traditions; all the emphasis on meditation is coming from the Far East. Nevertheless, they have brought meditation back to our attention.

In Gregorian chant, there are many modes called *meditationes*. Another word we use for the way the mind dwells on an idea is 'ruminate.' The word is derived from ruminant, which is an animal that chews the cud. So when someone insults you, often you'll *ruminate*, or chew on that insult for a while. But there is also a way of ruminating about high and sacred things having to do with prayer and meditation.

Recently, I asked myself: Have I really gotten the point where I don't have to be enslaved to anything? So I ruminated on going out of Egypt. Nobody can free themselves alone; but if I allow God to free me, then I can truly be free and leave Egypt. Everything that we have in our prayer is *zekher liy'tziyat Mitzrayim*, in memory of the Exodus from Egypt.

What does that mean? I take the *gestalt* from the story in Egypt and I import it, I lift it from that historical moment and import it into my life. That is a form of meditation in which I take something from our mythic history. Or, what was it like when we received the Torah, when there was such a breakthrough that our minds were blown, our egos were shattered, and we were able to *hear with our eyes* and *see with our ears?* That's synesthesia, right? When I go back to that place, I can spend time looking at that, and that's what contemplation is about.

There is also discursive meditation. Discursive meditation is giving myself a sermon. I say, "Zalman, is this the way want to live your life? Aren't there better things you could do?" I have an inner conversation with myself. When people aren't able to do that, they find it difficult to steer their lives. So you have a conversation with the many parts of yourself.

Sometimes you have to call an inner 'council.' There was a person by the name of Eligio Gallegos who was teaching people about totem animals. Every *chakra* has a different totem animal. You call them together and you have a conversation with them: *I have to make a decision. Will the wolf agree with me? Will the lion agree with me?* You try to get all the animals in council to agree.

When we have carved-out that inner space, we can then look at a series of ideas, and very often, lift them from the prayer book if we want. You can take up *Adon Olam asher Malakh b'terem kol y'tzir nivra,* "Master of the Universe, You ruled before there was anything created, and You will rule after all creation is consumed; You are from the beginning of the Big Bang to the last black hole." You can spend time sinking into that thought and expand your contemplation. When you do that, it moves from your head to your heart.

You can see such amazing pictures on the Internet. It is such a joy in a way. Someone sent me pictures from a new telescope that took pictures of galaxies. I tell you, it is such a busy cosmos. We think of space as being empty, but in reality, it is a busy place. When I allow myself to visualize that vastness, like in the opening credits of *Star Trek,* and to go with that in my meditation, I can see how vast the universe is. I can be conscious of that vastness, in which there are planets around the sun, and a galaxy around the solar system, and our galaxy is but one of many in the universe, and the universe is only a spin-off of the meta-verse which some people talk about! I can easily spend an hour contemplating this; it gets me into an awe which is called, *Yir'at Ha'Rom'mut,* the awe that comes from the vastness and the greatness, from the immensity of things.

In each of these meditative possibilities, I have to spend some time. The best way to do this is to plan ahead. If I want to take the next hour and do that discursive meditation, I'll begin with words, and then I'll let the words fade into images, and I'll let the images impinge on me.

I make up my mind about what I want to consider. I like the word 'consider.' In a business deal, you might ask, "For what consideration will you make the deal?" For how much money will we get a consideration? Consideration means, what will it mean to me to go into this contemplation. I plan it out: *I will pay attention to the vastness of the universe. I will pay attention to how this universe is constantly energized by Divinity. I will realize that I am a part of the universe being energized by Divinity, and I will go into a consideration of what that means to me in my life situation.*

Now that I have my plan, I can begin. But the meditatation may be a little too plain and dry if I don't begin with a melody. When you begin that way, a whole other thing happens inside.

As I said earlier, music changes how we hear the words. Most of our love songs would sound stupid if they didn't come with a melody. It is the same in *davvenen;* sometimes the words are not denotative, like a description of how to put a motorcycle together.

Do you remember the Robert Pirsig book, *Zen and The Art of Motorcycle Maintenance*? In it, Pirsig was trying to describe a quality. He points out that it is easy to give a description of something mechanical, but when you want to get to quality, it requires something deeper. You almost need to taste it, to have another kind of connection with it.

So I decide that I want to get into that meditation, to know that idea intimately, to love it, to feel it. For that I need connotative language, the kind I use in poetry, and so I begin with a melody.

We have such a range of melodies; it is a pity that 'yeshivah rock' has largely obscured them. Those rock melodies are easy to catch for celebrations, but have no meaning by themselves. Imagine I were to sing *Min Ha'Metzar*

Ha'Metzar to one of these Yeshivah Rock melodies; the words and the melody don't have a connection, because the Hebrew means: "Out of the constriction You have taken me, O Lord. You answered me and brought me to an expansiveness." For that, I need a different kind of melody.

The problem was, we needed to bring the young people in from the outside and they responded well to Yeshivah Rock. I can't blame them; I am also guilty of that. Over 50 years ago, I sometimes did Friday night services for young people with pre-recorded music by the NFTY Levites, a Reform youth group. The kids would dance in the semi-darkness and I would put on a strobe light. And the truth is, it was a way back into Judaism for many of the young people.

I call this approach to Jewish liturgy, 'wheelchair accessible.' It is a kind of spirituality that is so simple, it easy to get into as an audience or as a celebrator. We still do this to give people easy access to our prayer and celebration. But after a while, the people who have been to the 'wheelchair accessible' services are looking for something deeper. And that option often isn't available because we still want to accommodate the newcomers. There is a deeper yearning for more silence and deeper melodies of a different kind, like the Tzemah Tzedek's *D'veikut Niggun.* That is a melody for really getting close to God.

You have a sense with a melody like this that you are actually getting homesick for God. That is what such a melody does for you; it opens up the heart. If you have such a feeling going into the contemplation, then it isn't a mental thing anymore; it is something much, much deeper.

Repentence

When you are close to a melody, you come much closer to *t'shuvah*, repentance. Reb Pinhas of Koretz said:

121

"Why do people say that the *hazzan* (cantor) is a fool? Because the heavenly mansion of melody is very close to the mansion of *t'shuvah*; and if you are already at the mansion of melody, then why not go next door to the mansion of *t'shuvah*? So if the *hazzan* doesn't do that, he is a fool." So you see, melodies are made to get us to the place of *t'shuvah*.

Part of *t'shuvah* is regret. I like the word regret. Regret that has the sense of pulling back: *With all my heart, I would like to make what I shouldn't have done un-happen.* Most of the time I can't. I can't make things that have happened *un-happen,* but that sense of regret, going back, and turning around is connected to *t'shuvah,* returning to God. We feel: *What can I do? I don't want to be cut off from God; I don't want to be opaque to God. What happens if I did something that wasn't right?*

Most people can get into a place of thinking, *I'll never be able to fix it, because look what I did.* But we have to understand from the start that this world is a world in which we are meant to learn by our mistakes; there is no other way to learn. Biologically, we can learn only from mistakes. Schools don't give you a chance to do that; they want you to learn by the transfer of information. But we learn by exploration and observing the results. That is why you need labs in physics and chemistry, so you can make mistakes and learn from them.

We are made in such a way that we can't learn unless we make mistakes. Sigmund Freud's *super-ego* is a false conscience; it is not the real conscience. The false conscience says that you are not supposed to make a mistake! But Freud's *ego* is more realistic, saying, "If you can make mistakes, you can learn from them." On the other hand, the *super-ego* says, "You made a mistake: for that you will suffer for the rest of your life."

When I think about what was built into the universe, prior to anything else, I am reminded of the beginning of

Genesis: "The spirit of God hovered above the waters."*
The Midrash says that was *t'shuvah*, the possibility of returning, the possibility of correcting. Rabbi Nahman of
Bratzlav put it this way: "If you believe you can spoil,
you must believe you can fix"

People often fail to see that this fixing is simply part
of the ongoing work of spirituality. They think that this is
just something that you need to do on Rosh Hashanah
and Yom Kippur. Even in the middle of a regular day,
there can be a moment of *t'shuvah: Okay, God! I made a
mistake; I'd like to know how to fix it.* If we made ourselves
more conscious of this need, we would apologize much
sooner to the people we hurt.

It is the same way with how we use our bodies, in the
sense of recognizing the occasions for sin. Catholics used
to talk about avoiding occasions for sin. If I know that
doughnuts are not good for me, then I know where I
shouldn't be going. If I have been there already, at least I
can make sure to say, "Okay, from now on, I won't go to
the bakery." I can program what I am going to do, and I
have choice over that. That is where *t'shuvah* comes in.
When we do something wrong in action, we need to fix it
in action. I am talking about action, speech, and thought.

When we do something wrong in action with an object, with something that has to do with activity, we have
to go and fix it in that place. It can't be fixed in another
place. If I have to fix something that I did in speech, in
relationship, then I have to go back to the place of speech
and relationship and confront the other person with my
apology. It isn't always easy to do, because we often have
the sense that we will be rebuffed; we have the feeling
that the person may not want to talk to us. But when you
do so directly and show them that this is not a ploy, it
can make a real difference.

---

* Genesis 1:2.

We have seen so many politicians and other public figure making these public apologies. You have a sense that this is merely a political strategy. It doesn't seem entirely real. When it is real, you say: "I am so sorry. I am sorry that I hurt you." It is direct. Another factor is learning to forgive. If I learn to forgive another person, I don't feel so badly about going to apologize, because I have experienced what it feels like.

The first time I apologize and say, "I'm sorry," it is not likely to take the pain away; but it may make it possible for me to talk to that person again. This is called s'lihah, making an overture. It is not m'hilah, a correction. I am saying, "Excuse me, I did wrong; I would like to make it up to you." That is the first part of the apology. And with God it is the same way too. "I recognize that I didn't do this one right; I am sorry." The second part is: How can I correct this? This is called the m'hilah, and is like mahol, a dance. It is a chance to let me look at it from the other perspective and see what it is like. I take your place, you take my place for a moment, and we work it out.

Finally there is a KaPPaRah that not only fixes what needs fixing, but creates a deeper relationship between the two of us afterwards. That is why we speak of Yom KiPPuR. By that time we have done the s'lihot in Ellul, and on Rosh Hashanah we have done m'hilah, and Yom Kippur completes it with kapparah, which deals with the deepest part of forgiveness and reconciliation.

When we recognize our basic fallibility, and we have a sense that God has programmed us so that we should be able to make mistakes and learn from them, and that we are being supported in that, then when we feel regret t'shuvah begins to work. It won't change anything unless we become aware of our motives. I may say, "I'm sorry." I may talk about all kinds of things with the other person, but things won't change unless I know what was the motive, what it was that triggered me, that got me to say that nasty thing in the first place: *Where was I coming from? What was my pain?* Unless I dig a little deeper, the *t'shuvah* is not going to be real. It is only going to be external. If I don't know the motivation, I won't know what the real problem was, and I will most probably repeat it because I haven't found the cause yet.

The thing that is really important to recognize is that if I have to go and apologize to someone, I am not going alone; God is going with me. I have to have the sense that I won't be able to make any of these amends unless I have divine help. Remember that we are made fallible! If we are made fallible, then even the apology will be fallible. If I really want it to work, I have to work with that knowledge.

Eighth Talk
Spiritual Maturity & Socialized Meditation

It is so important not to rush. When I sing a *niggun* before *davvenen,* I am sometimes tempted to sing it faster in order to get to my prayer. Then it hits me how stupid that is, because it is so good in the middle of the *niggun;* why should I rush? When I start thinking about the compulsion we have when it comes to *davvenen*—to rush, rush, rush—it seems more important not to be seduced into producing a quantity of words mindlessly, but to give attention to the moment when you are right there in God's presence instead. Why rush through it? Where you are is good.

When Reb Zushe of Anipol* was studying Talmud, he would stay on one page for months, until people asked him, "Why are you staying on this one page and not going on?" He answered, "Why should I go further if where I am feels right?"

On any level of spiritual work it is important not to rush. It is important to be really *there,* and not to think of what comes next, to distract oneself from the present moment. I think that's another meaning of *kavvanah.*

Spiritual Ups and Downs

There is a fallacy that comes from taking our spiritual attitude from the book of Deuteronomy, from treating it literally. We then fall into an error. The error consists in thinking that once you are on a certain level in your spiritual life, you will always be on that level: *I have achieved*

---

* Rabbi Zushe of Anipol (d. 1800) was a disciple of the Maggid of Mezritch.

this particular rung, this spiritual level, and I will always be here. This is a mistake. How can I say that I will always be there? If anything is happening in the spiritual life, it is dynamic and has its ups-and-downs.

We always have to be in the present moment. There is such a difference in the texture of time between Pesah and Tisha b'Av, between Purim and Yom Kippur. We cannot expect to experience them in the same place.

There's a profound teaching by Reb Shneur Zalman of Liadi. In the preface to the second book of the *Tanya*, he speaks of the distinction between human beings and Angels based on a sentence in the Bible. He points out that an Angel is called a "standing one," one who stands on one straight leg. On the other hand, a human being is called one who walks. A human being has two legs and bobs up and down in walking. *Hesed* and *Gevurah*, up and down, right and left. He further says, "Seven times will a *tzaddik* fall and yet rise." So to expect that this won't be a roller coaster in matters of spirit—forget it!

The Progression of the Spirit

Let's take a look at a kind of progression of the spirit. I heard this from a remarkable person, Dr. Karl Stern, who explained it to me in the language of Freud's theory of psychosexual development.[*]

According to Freud, a baby is all in the mouth. This is the *oral stage;* it wants to absorb and take in. What does a baby want? Mother's milk. What is the best description that the Torah has of mother's milk? I'll lead you into a "land of milk and honey."[**]

It is so wonderful when a person first gets touched by spirit. I am not necessarily talking about people born into

---

[*] Dr. Karl Stern (1906-1975) was a German-Canadian psychologist and convert to Catholicism.

[**] Exodus 3:8.

religious families, where they got that nourishment from the mother's milk; but when someone becomes a *ba'al t'shuvah*, they really want to get into it. It is an experience that it feels so good, they think: *Now I have finally found my place, a place that nurtures my soul; I know exactly what I am getting, and it is truly good.*

Back to the late '60s, people who would say: "I'm into this now—It's out of sight, far out! It's the greatest spirituality that you can get." If you were to meet that guy a half a year later, he would tell you, "I found a *really* great *guru*; his *shaktipat* (transfer of spiritual energy) is *way* more powerful than the one I had before."

You see, there are some folks who go from place to place, continually looking for a holy chocolate fix. If they find it in Judaism, they'll stay for a while, but will move on when it's time for them to enter the next phase. They will go on to something or someone else who will give them the same kind of a rush. That is an *oral stage* fixation. They always want to be fed: "God give me a little grace." God gives them a little grace, and they say, "I want more."

After a while, we come to the Freudian *anal stage,* where you need discipline, a kind of spiritual potty training. You know that you cannot relieve yourself just anywhere. At this point begins the learning of the basic moral guidelines, and with it the building of the *super-ego.*

At the anal stage, some people get fixated on very strict observance in religion. Most fundamentalists are fixated there because they have the need to believe in the inerrancy of Scripture: *In Scripture, there is nothing wrong, and if anything is wrong, it is because I'm not heeding what it tells me to do.* If they ask, "How do I understand the Bible?" The answer is: "Never mind; it is not for you and your small mind to interpret it. Just read and take it straight. We'll tell you how to do it." Fundamentalism says: "Who the hell are you to change *halakhah,* to change

129

the law? How dare you do this in the face of such great *gedolim,* halakhic authorities!" Then they tell me about the greatness and loyalty of past generations. This is a lot of what goes on in Judaism in certain quarters.

After a while, if you've done the disciplines and you are really good at it, so you don't have to pay attention to it anymore. You start looking for meaning, for beauty, and for symbolism. This is what the Freudians called the *phallic stage: Oh boy! This is so great. There are so many thresholds to go through, and the* mezuzzah *has to be at every threshold. My eyes have to have a* mezuzzah, *my nose, my ears have to have a* mezuzzah. In this way, and with great enthusiasm, they go into this whole wonderful area of symbolism. They say, "This is so great, and look at all the meaning we have available to us." The whole Passover *seder* is built on that—*matzah zu sh'anu okhlin.* 'Why do we eat *matzah?'* We examine the ritual object and its meaning and get the kids to ask questions about it. The whole *Haggadah* takes this perspective.

To be in the world of symbols is great, and you often spend a lot of time there. There are some people who are spiritual aesthetes, always looking for better spiritual champagne, seeing themselves as spiritual connoisseurs. They say, "Yes, yes the *Missa Solemnis* of Mozart is much better than Yosselle Rosenblatt." I sympathize with them because it is a good place to be. It is enchanting. With this aesthetic view, you see things with more dimensionality and this is wonderful. The problem is that you can also get stuck there. The worst example of someone stuck in symbolism is Nero fiddling while Rome is burning. He doesn't understand what pain is being caused to the people.

Then comes a new level of spirituality, one that cares for other people. This is like Freud's *latency stage.* There are some people who join with the prophet Isaiah and say: What need have I of your sacrifices? Your hands are full of blood. What I really care for is that you find the hungry and bring them into your house, take care of the homeless, and help them. Do you think I want or need your fast, for you to trouble your stomach? Trouble your conscience instead, and keep your conscience clean.* At this point, it is no longer ritual, a specific devotion to God, but it is what serves God when you are doing for other people. Then your spiritual light breaks forth and your soul's healing takes place.

There is a story about Reb Moshe Leib Sassover who disappeared during s'lihot: **

There was a Litvak (Lithuanian) who asked the Hasidim, "Where is the Rebbe?" They said that the Rebbe is now saying his prayers in heaven. The Litvak is like someone from Missouri—"Show me." So he stalks the Rebbe and sees him come out of his house wearing peasant clothes. He goes into the forest with a rope and an axe in his hand. He picks up fallen wood, breaks it up with the axe, and ties it into a bundle which he puts on his shoulder. Then the Rebbe goes into town to an old broken down shack at the end of the shtetl. He knocks on the door, and an old woman's voice calls out, "Who is it?" The Rebbe, posing as a Polish peasant says: "It is I, Voitek. I brought you some wood." She says, "I have no money to pay you." He says, "You have a good God. You will pay me soon enough." She says that she can't get out of bed to make a fire. And he says, "So I will make it for you." And while he is lighting the fire, he is reciting the penitential prayers of s'lihot. The Litvak comes back and someone says, "Where is the Rebbe?" Someone else answers, "He is in heaven." The our Litvak says, "If not higher."

This is such a wonderful story because it talks about this level where the concern is for the people.

_____

* Isaiah 1:10-17.

** Rabbi Moshe Leib of Sassov (1745-1807), a disciple of Shmelke of Nikholsburg.

131

There is another story about Rabbi Israel Salanter who was once invited to the home of a person who said, "Rebbe, we have such a wonderful *Shabbat* table.* We sit till midnight at the table and sing and celebrate and have such wonderful Torah conversation." Reb Israel says: "I'm sorry, I can't sit with you so long; I need to go to sleep early. I can only make it if you promise that you will be done by 10 o'clock." His host promises, and so the *rebbe* comes. Finally, 10 o'clock arrives and he is about to leave when the woman who works in the kitchen comes out to him and says: "Thank you holy rabbi for finishing early. I have been working since before dawn to make a *Shabbat*. When they sit till midnight and then I have to clean up afterwards, I get so tired. Thank you for finishing earlier."

Here you have such a wonderful example of someone who is willing to let go of the symbolic celebration for the sake of another human being.

In another story, the same Rabbi Israel is very sparing as he washes his hands before the meal. His host says, "Rabbi, you can use more water." But the rabbi says: "This water has to be brought all the way up the hill from the river by a person who works very hard; I do not wish to be pious on his back."

This is how the human dimension and a concern for other people is considered a great a way of the service to God. That is the service of the *latency stage*.

Stories keep coming up and demand to be told:

A man came before Pesah to ask Rabbi Hayyim Brisker if he can fulfill the commandment to drink the four cups by drinking milk.** Rabbi Hayyim says, "No," and hands the man 20 rubles. The Brisker Rav's wife

---

* Rabbi Yisrael Lipkin (1810-1883), known as Rabbi Yisrael Salanter, father of the Mussar Movement.

** Rabbi Hayyim HaLevi Soloveitchik (1853-1918), known as Rabbi Hayyim Brisker, creator of the Brisker approach to talmudic study.

says: "But you *may* do it that way; it *is* kosher. So why did you give him the money?" Rabbi Hayyim points out that it was clear that he did not have the money for *fleishig* (meat) for his *seder*. Since one may not mix meat and milk, Rabbi Hayyim realized that the man didn't have enough money to provide for a real *seder* meal.

These levels of concern for other people have to do with the stage of latency. That is where we care more for the *hevrah*.

There is another level a person gets to where they are really not interested in much social connection with human beings, but seek only what is sacred and holy. It is like Reb Shneur Zalman of Liadi who said: *Ribbono shel Olam*, "Master of the Universe, I don't want your paradise; I don't want your world to come; I want You, You, You." This is like saying that all this that I've experienced and seen is like a shimmer, a dream. What really counts is to flow into God like a drop flows into the ocean.

This is a very high level. Most of us will take several incarnations until we will make it to that place. It is very important to recognize that when you are in one stage, and saying, "This is the way spirituality should be," that it is just a stage. In the oral stage, tasting the spiritual chocolate seems like everything. But then someone in the anal stage comes along and says, "Be sure you keep your discipline." They will fight and argue about which is the right way, and each one will claim that they have the answer. The truth is that they are both stages in the process of the journey of the soul. Nor is it necessarily hierachical. So I just wanted to get rid of the fallacy of stability.

Booting the Right Software

Now I want to review a little bit: How do we prepare for *davvenen*? If I want to do something on the computer, I have to boot the right software. How many times do people go to *davven* without having 'booted' the right software? But first, you have to possess the right software. What would be the right software for getting into *davvenen*?

When I begin with a *niggun*, I am making a good beginning. I sing phrases that offer gentle devotion to God: *I want to give You this love that I feel at this moment.* That is best expressed with a melody. That's one level of booting the software. You know for yourself which *niggun* turns you on. Then there are stories, and you may know a good story. You know that when you review that story in your mind, then you will go and *davven* much better because of it.

I'll resist the temptation at this point to start telling illustrative stories, but they are around. Besides the stories that you hear about other people, you can also tune into your own stories, to past theophanies you have had. What do I mean?

There are moments when I tell myself one of those stories, or rehearse one of the insights I have gotten, and I get to the place where I feel a stirring of excitement and I say again, *"Aha!"* I feel the delight of the original theophany. I need to recall it first, because theophanies come and go, and most of them get lost because we don't put them in a vessel. To put it in the language of computers; we don't give it a filename and decide which folder to keep it in. And that's very important.

When I start *davvenen,* I can take some insight from before, and call that into my *davvenen.* Now I have a story, and I have a *niggun.* By that time I am sensitized to the words printed in the *siddur* that I may not have been sensitive to before. On the inside, I am opening up and saying that these 'tangents' touching on the words of prayer will be important.

Now, another thing: You have an encounter with a special person, and you remember the taste of that encounter. For instance, when I think of how my *rebbe* davvened, I can almost see and hear and feel him. If I tune into that before I *davven* my own prayer, it would change how I prayed. When people say, "The prayer book doesn't turn me on," I want to say, "The book *doesn't* turn you on; it's your task to turn on the book." You have to go to those modalities, so that whatever is in the book will light up a significant place in your heart and soul.

You have to 'log-on' to the longing. It is so hard to talk about the longing without getting a sense of infantile selfishness. There is an element of regression inside of me in which I become the baby that was not held enough by mama. That 'baby-longing' may be one of the fibers in the cable of longing. But there are other places of longing in which we say, *Ha'levay*, "Oh, that it should only be ideal." We have that picture in which we long for how we want it to be when *Mashiah* comes.

When we think of the capacity that Earth has for communication, and the ability we have to share with one another, we can imagine how we might live as an organism together. For instance, what if the Senate would act like an organ of the body, concerned for the health of the whole? If we lived in this organismic way, how wonderful it would be. Once I have a look at that, I feel a longing for that possibility: Oy! *If only* — ha'levay — *if only* . . . So that longing has to be brought into the *davvenen* too, because that's how I nurture the longing.

Davvenen in the Vernacular

At this point, I want to talk about why you should also *davven* in the vernacular, even if you know Hebrew, and even if you are fluid with the *siddur*, and you can translate every word in it. If you have not davvened in the vernacular, you haven't really gotten to what the *siddur* is about. There are images that you won't get from the *siddur* alone. For instance, you go up on a mountain facing East; it is still night, and you wait for the dawn. Finally, the sun comes over the horizon and it feels like such a miracle, and you say: *Ha'me'ir la'aretz v'ladarim aleha b'rahamim,* "You, God, are illumining the world and all who dwell there with compassion." Having been on the mountain, the next time you say those words it will have an overtone of what you've seen on the mountain, and your prayer will be enriched by that experience.

The vernacular does two things.

There is 'high language,' like in the Episcopal *Book of Common Prayer.* That prayer book is a remarkable document, because it is as if you are dealing with God as you would deal with an actual king in his court. If you look at cathedrals, they are all made as if the throne is the altar; people come in and genuflect in front of the throne. They also use a language that is very formal. They don't want to break down and cry when they address "His Majesty, the King." They want to do this in a very special and formal way. But when your heart is breaking and you want to talk to God, you want to cry. You wouldn't be using formal language like "vouchsafe, O Lord" and "bestow upon us." It would be more *Oy! Tatte zisser,* "Sweet, compassionate Father of the orphans, Protector of the widows; take a look where we are, at what *tzores* we have!" You see, in Yiddish, it was easy to do that, and we never complained about someone who would *davven* like this in Yiddish. So why should we have a problem with English, or any other vernacular?

In fact, there was a special *siddur* called *Korban Minhah Siddur* in which the Hebrew was translated into Yiddish for women's *davvenen.* Then there were many other collections of women's prayers called *T'khinnes,* 'supplications.' They would have headings like: "The Prayer of a Wife for a Husband Who is Away on a Business Trip, that He May Come Home Safe," or "The Prayer of a Mother for Her Children." These special prayers offered models for people who otherwise might find themselves speechless. They might wonder: *What can I say? I don't know enough to talk to God!* But they could open the book and see: *"Oy! Ribbono shel Olam,* my husband is on the road; please have pity on him and get him home safely."

You see, it legitimizes her own thoughts and tells her that it is okay to address God directly for these things. It is a simple and direct language of the heart, and the one which she speaks on a daily basis.

If I were to use the King James English for "He leadeth me beside the still waters" and "Yea, though I walk through the valley of the shadow of death,"* I don't have the same panic that I would have when they put me on the gurney and are about to take me into the operating room. In that situation, I am in no way able to use fancy language; I need to communicate urgently and directly with God.

For this reason, I worked very hard to create a weekday *siddur* in the vernacular.** If you have this *siddur*, the best way to make use of it is to sit and read through the whole thing, but not all at once. If you haven't read through the whole *siddur*, you don't know where the places are that turn you on.

The first time you read it, read it out loud so you can hear it; otherwise you won't get the feeling behind the words. Then highlight passages of special significance to you, or passages where you want to remember people in need of healing. For instance, "Healer of all flesh who does wondrous things," to which I would add another translation, "who creates spontaneous remissions."

If you have highlighted some of these, and you know which passages you would like to use, you also know the time-limit that constrains you. You will go ahead and stick with that limit, emphasizing the passages you need for today. It won't be the same another day, because each day you will pick another one of those highlighted passages closer to your feelings that day.

---

* Psalms 23:2,4.

** *Sh'ma': A Concise Weekday Siddur for Praying in English.*

Dealing with Constraints

There was a time when I was working with teenagers in Jewish summer camps, and I would go from one bunk to another telling the campers, "Today you have twelve minutes to complete your morning prayers." Another morning, I might give them eighteen minutes. I never gave them more than twenty minutes, because I wanted them to feel that they could really accomplish that every day, and that they had their own choice what to omit and what to include. There were some people there—good observant people—who objected to my restriction for the campers; they didn't realize that if I insisted that they do the entire service as printed in the prayer book, they wouldn't be doing it once they returned from camp and went back to school.

If you then say, "This is the time I have, and this is the time I want to devote to it," you create the preparation that I was talking about before.

Sometimes people who can't get out of the house and go to *shul* to observe a *yahrzeit*, would still like to *davven Ma'ariv* in solitude at home and say *Kaddish* for their loved ones. For this reason, I created an evening and morning service on video in which there is a whole *kehillah*, a whole community *davvenen Ma'ariv*, and you are invited to say the *Kaddish* when the time comes and you can *davven* along. I have done the same for *Shaharit*, and I think that's an important possibility for people in general; because when you have grown used to it, doing your own *davvenen* along with the video, it could be a good refresher. For shut-ins and people in the homes for the aged that would be a wonderful way of participating in communal prayer.

Socialized Meditation

It is important to recognize that, for most people, *davvenen* will not be a reality unless they have learned to do it in, at least in, *two-sies,* that is to say, with another person.

I once wrote an article called "Between Solo and Minyan." When you look at the way in which it usually goes, if you only have eight people, it is not a *minyan.** So everyone is expected to separate and *davven* on their own. I disagree with that attitude, because when three people eat together they have a *mezumman.*** If you have ten people and six are *davvenen* and four are not (but are there to help them make a *minyan),* you can repeat the *Amidah* out loud. So you see that there are numbers *between* one and ten.

Sometimes I like to talk about 'transpersonal sociology.' What would the *minyan* of my dreams look like? In the past, I have had occasions with some students to experiment with this kind of *minyan.* We would stand in the positions that are on the Tree of Life. This one was in the *Keter,* that one in *Hokhmah,* another in *Binah* — everyone had a place. Then everyone had to contribute something from their place on the tree to the *minyan.* Certain prayers were earmarked for each *sefirah.* It was a wonderful thing because we were so in ensemble together that I could understand how *minyan* really works. There is a place when everything is plugged-in in the right way and the lights go on. They say the *Shekhinah* is present where ten are gathered to *davven;* if they davvened in such a way that they create an ensemble of ten *sefirot,* with those attitudes and ways of functioning together, I have no doubt that the Presence is there.

But I think it can happen between two people also, between three people, four, five, six, and seven is a wonderful number. You can do it in so many ways.

---

* With nine, we start counting the Torah scroll.

** A quorum of three people whose presence is necessary for the public recitation of Grace after Meals.

I want to begin with the *two-sie,* because the heart needs to have an *other* to talk to. When you have a way of feeling the other person, you get into what Martin Buber called the *I-Thou* relationship. Some years ago, it was the 10th *yahrzeit* of Martin Buber in 1975, and a number of us met in Washington D.C. under the leadership of Art Waskow.* It was wonderful. Some people gave papers on Buber and his thought, but I wanted to do an "*I-Thou* lab." It is easy to say that *I-Thou* is better than *I-It,* but how do you do it? What do you have to do inside of yourself in order to get to that *I-Thou* place? We had an *I-Thou* lab.

Ani ma'amin b'emunah shlemah, I truly believe that in the center of my being—which I call the *heart*—is a sanctuary where the *Shekhinah* resides. Imagine that I want to talk to God, to the *Shekhinah.* I'm not trying to turn to Jerusalem; I'm not going 'up there' or 'out there,' because I know it is *inside.* Nevertheless, it is very hard for me to pray to the God within me. The chief reason is that the ego stands at the door and says, "You mean *me;* you mean *me;* you mean *me.*" It is much easier if I can say to you: "Would you do me a favor? I have a real a real concern which I need to bring to God; would you allow me to address God in His sanctuary within you? Please move your ego aside for a moment as I look into your eyes and go to the One who dwells in your heart. I want to say, 'Please send a speedy healing to Malkah bat Shoshanah. *Amen*' "

Given your assent, that goes so much easier, because I connect by looking into your eyes. Along with that goes an affirmation, that what I see is another aspect, another face that God is wearing. Can you imagine if two people were to do this in the morning or at night before they go to sleep? A husband and wife could address the God within the other. How wonderful!

---

* Rabbi Arthur Waskow is the founder of The Shalom Center, which addresses political issues from a liberal Jewish perspective.

I often try to show people that they approach and hold the *siddur* in the wrong way. You come to *shul*, and for the tenth time, you read the introduction to the prayer book because you're bored with it. If it would tell you something that you hadn't encountered before, you would be more interested in it, right? But you read it week after week, and it becomes really boring. If, on the other hand, when I come to the words *Nishmat kol hai t'varekh et shimkha*, "the soul of every living being praises You, O Lord,"* I say to my partner, "I'll do the audio for a while, and you do the video, and then we'll switch." Then I start reading and you, at that point, don't have to bother holding a book or getting words out of the book. All that you need to do is create the virtual scene in your awareness—of the soul, the breath of everything that lives. With the in-breath, it breathes you in. With the out-breath, it breathes you out. The whole world, all living beings . . . Look what kind of a symphony is going on through all the levels of being. You do that in your video. Then when I finish with a paragraph, I hand you the *siddur*, and you read to me and I go to that place.

I call that 'socialized meditation,' because we are sharing the meditation. In that way, we can get to places where neither of us could go alone.

Another exercise I developed for the *I-Thou* lab was this: I begin a sentence and you finish it. Then you begin a sentence and I finish it. Neither of us knows what's actually going to happen. Someone do this with me:

Reb Zalman: The purpose of this exercise is . . .

Participant: To explore my inner world. I'm a little of afraid that you are going to see within me that . . .

---

* *Shabbat* liturgy.

Reb Zalman: You are, first of all, fully alive in a region that many people are asleep in. For this, I give thanks, because it will bring you to . . .

Participant: A place where I'm actually able to honor that part of me. I'm really excited to have this conversation with you because . . .

Reb Zalman: It is not one mind doing it; it is two minds together. And when two people are together then . . .

Participant: Our combination is greater than the sum of its parts.

Reb Zalman: Amen.

This is a wonderful to partner. If you pick a topic, saying, "Now we are going to talk about *Shabbat* . . . about *mitzvot* . . . about the month of Adar . . ." Whatever you want to talk about, you say: "We'll start this conversation and try and follow that track. I don't know what you are going to say, and you don't know what I'm going to say. We are doing a *together-ing.*" That's something we can do in *two-sies.*

There are other things that you can do with larger groups. I have taken people, even very large groups, and had them line up according to their birthdays on the calendar. We'd start with January and end with December in the circle. This creates a sociogram based on the Zodiac. What would this do to the House of Representatives and the Senate if all the Aquarians and all the Leos were sitting together, regardless of their party affiliation? That could be such a wonderful way to work together.

Many *b'rokhes* to you for your *davvenen* together, and that you may have enjoyment in some of the things I have talked about. *Shalom, shalom — kol tuv.*

Question and Answer Session

Question: I find that I am not turned-on by my own prayer anymore. I am unable to access my pain because I feel numb; but in groups, I am often turned-on by the emotionality of the group. But if I were to really to let out all of my pain, I would scream at the top of my lungs. I don't feel safe doing that, even at a Jewish Renewal synagogue. It would be too explosive. By myself, I don't feel it; but with others, it is too much. I wrestle with this.

Reb Zalman: Soon I will be leading *davvenen* at Nevei Kodesh. We will start at 6:30 in the morning with learning, and then there will be a *minyan* with Torah reading. Obviously, on an ordinary Friday night, you wouldn't want to let out your pain in a service; but what would it be like if we were to have a vigil on Tisha b'Av night? That's the real time for it. Most of us don't do *Tikkun Hatzot*, but if we were to do that midnight lament, then that would also be a place to come and let out that primal scream. So, some of this has to do with the calendar, but I'll tell you something: if you needed to do this, and you called me and a couple of other friends whom you like, I would be with you to 'midwife' that expression.

Question: I was thinking about the levels you were talking about at the beginning: how do you know what level you are on? And if you are stuck, how do you get unstuck and move to another level?

Reb Zalman: Well, let me start with the last one. If you are stuck, how do you get un-stuck? There is a statement the Rabbis make: "Anybody who is in chains can't free himself." It is always necessary for someone else to help you. Without a challenge from outside, you may stay fixated in any of these levels.

Let's say you have become very anal and meticulous, and I ask you: "What do you think about God? What kind of a God is watching to see which fingernail you cut first, and which one you cut second? Have you had any beautiful experiences to share with God? Have you had more beautiful experiences *of* God?" Then you bring them out of that and say, "Every one of your observances carries this possibility; there is something beautiful within it, and you have to try and find it." It's a challenge. You can break the same challenge latter on and say: "You have all this wonderful aesthetic, this holy aesthetic. When was the last time you were in a soup kitchen and helped out?" In each case, the challenge is there, eating away at the pattern in which you are stuck.

Question: When you were holding the book open and talking about directing your words to the face of an actual person, I was remembering a time when I was at services and looking around at people with their books. And I was thinking that it might be better to just have mirrors in the book. Today when you were speaking, I was thinking of mirrors, but not just mirrors to look back at me, but almost turning the book to have my friend in the mirror. I wonder what you have to say about this. When we start to do that too much, we might lose contact with what is there. Or we start to do what is in the book too much and never reflect back, or reflect on our friend. How can we work with balancing that?

Reb Zalman: It is clear that this is necessary, right? There is a beautiful statement in the book of Ecclesiastes (3:1), "For everything there is a season." Sometimes it time for this, and sometimes it is a time for that. Remember when they had biorhythms? Sometimes you're above the line, sometimes below the line. It has to move this way. I think the recognition that it depends on the time, the situation, and what's being called for. Think about it in an organic way, like an organism. If your toe wants something, it doesn't have to fill out a request in triplicate; you deal with it directly because that's what is important; that is how a body responds.

Ninth Talk
Dancing for God & Being with God

There used to be a time when I served as a *shohet* in the morning, and in the afternoon, I would teach children in the Talmud Torah. This was all while I was serving as a rabbi in Fall River, Massachusetts. So you can imagine how I needed a transition before teaching the children after I had spent the morning slaughtering chickens. To do this, I would lock myself in the office before class and put on a five-minute recording of a Greek *hassapiko* — it sounded very much like a good klezmer tune — and dance to it. That helped me transition from one place to another.

People feel funny about being seen when they dance alone. It always makes you feel a little uneasy. Is it crazy to dance by yourself? When David danced before the Lord, his wife, Michal didn't get it; she thought he was desporting himself before the women of the town, and didn't forgive him easily. Then the *TaNaKh* tells, she was barren and didn't bear children.

Right now I'm thinking of the people who don't understand what it means to be in ecstasy, or to be dancing in a trance-state. But even if someone is not engaged in that deep form of dance, something happens in dance to take the body out of its lock. Even when you are singing, the body wants to participate. That's why people *shuckle* or sway in prayer; they make these gestures because they are filled with emotion.

We don't hear *hazzanim* much any more. When the classical *hazzan* would begin a *recitativo*, people would listen and hum along. They would give him a chord, usually a minor, and he would go into curlicues and falsettos. A *hazzen* was what they called an *Omed kinstler*, meaning an artist at the prayer stand. When they had someone like this, he was able to take the words to such places that the people would begin to feel them.

One thing that gives me a lot of joy is to dance for God when nobody else is looking. You wouldn't want to do this in public unless you were really a good dancer; but I tell you, I've seen some people dance prayers very beautifully; it is like a mime. A mime is not interested in having you tell them, "You're doing good" or "You're not doing good." The mime is disconnected from you and alone in their own world. In the same way, I've seen some spiritual dancers do that.

It is really important for us to take some time, when nobody else is around, set the lights low, and say, "I want to dance with You, God." It sounds funny when I say that because I imagine a response from people, "What do you mean?" But where else would the romance between my soul and God be clearer than in such a dance?

When you do this a few times, what happens is that the next time get into regular *davvenen,* there's going to be some body memory that will come back. Sometimes it will express itself in a gesture; sometimes it will express itself in a sigh, or in the emphasis on a word; because that's how the body would respond and help out. I wanted to talk about that, because I think it is important that people should also approach *davvenen* in a way that transcends words, spending time with *niggunim* and movement.

I think that it would be wonderful for people to write new religious poetry. We are stuck with the poetry of the Middle Ages, and some of the *piyyutim* that we have, even when you know Hebrew well, is very difficult to penetrate. Yehuda HaLevi, Shlomo ibn Gabirol, and the author of the *L'kha Dodi* and *Yedid Nefesh,* made it easier for us to tune in to the exaltation. Even in our on day, I remember how I felt when I first heard George Harrison's "My Sweet Lord." Like a contemporary *Yedid Nefesh*, which says, "I want to see your beauty," it says, "I really want to see you" *Lord*. To think that Jewish music is confined to Slavic music from Eastern Europe is a mistake. We have music from Spain, Ladino music you can listen to in wonderful varieties. The Yemenites and the Syrian Jews and the Baghdadi Jews all sing differently; the Moroccan sing differently. They all have wonderful melodies which come from the land they had adopted. Should it be any different here?

On my first visit to Colorado, I came to the Stanley Hotel in Estes Park. I was there with two other presenters; B'nai B'rith had a retreat there and we were scholars in residence. They gave me the *kavod* to do *Kiddush* and I began to sing the blessing. Soon, people start to giggle because they recognized I was using the tune to "Home on the Range." They didn't understand what I really wanted to say, which was that this is American western tune and *Shabbat* is a time "where seldom is heard a discouraging word and the sky is not cloudy all day."

We have always taken from the music of the land, as much as some would like to deny it. I think about the sad melodies of the *kretchma*, the Russian roadhouse that filtered into Hasidism, of how the Bobover Hasidim sing central Europe melodies in major keys.

Some people used to say about American music, or the music of other cultures, "No, this is not our music." Who used to say that? The old-timers who never experienced the new music in feeling; they had an allergy to the music that wasn't the music that they knew; and they also had a terrible allergy to other religions.

Other Houses of Worship

In the past, when I would visit another house of worship, I wanted to see how they did their ritual and liturgy, how they did their God-work. And my experience, almost every time, was that I would say to myself: "Oh, how beautifully these people worship. *Oy!* How I have to improve what I am doing." It wasn't that I wanted to become them; it was that in comparison I could see parallel structures and appreciate the different emphases. And that gave me insight into how I could make little shifts.

Returning to the topic of Freud's five stages as applied to religion, a lot of what happens in other religious services has to do with symbolism. You come into a Hindu temple and you ring a bell to announce yourself. While we say, *Mah tovu ohalekha Ya'akov.* The Catholic purifies with a little holy water and makes the sign of the cross. We all have interesting ways of entering the sacred space.

As I watch how other liturgies progress, I see that wherever the liturgy has grown organically, it has a way of going up, coming to a summit, and then coming down. If you watch our *davvenen,* you see the same thing: *Birkhat Ha'Shahar, P'sukei d'Zimrah, Kriyat Sh'ma', Sh'ma', Amidah,* and then you come down. If you look at that curve, you see that it is very much like a masculine sexual curve. It builds up, up, up, up, up, and then goes down very fast. On the feminine side, it wouldn't necessarily go that way. It would come down much gentler afterwards, and take it in deeper. It takes longer.

I feel that when people say, "How come God doesn't answer my prayer?" it is because they hang up too soon. There isn't time taken on the way down. What am I supposed to do on the way down? I have to remember what happened on the way up that touched me; I don't want to forget. When I'm climbing down the ladder, I'm plucking all the fruit that ripened on my way up, so that I can take it back with me and invest it in the day that I'm about to have.

Let's say I had an insight on the way up: "How wonderful it is for people to have a God who fills them with life." Now I want to take it back with me when I come down. So I commit myself to remembering that, and where I was at when I received it, a couple of times a day. That is taking the fruit of the *davvenen* and bringing it down.

So the structure goes higher and higher and then comes down. When I watch a Roman Catholic Mass, I say, "See, they also have that!" In most of the more liberal services I go to, they never seem to go up. That means that you have never have a spiritual orgasm. You have to go through the build-up to the point of release, and having experienced that point, you want to come down and take along everything that has happened. You can see that in certain worship situations like in the traditional Jewish liturgy, in the Roman Catholic Mass, and the Greek Orthodox Mass.

When I am downtown on Pearl Street around noontime, I may chance to see a man get on his knees and say the Muslim *Fatihah*, unashamed of doing this in front of all the people there. It gives me such respect for him. And when I come back to start *davvenen*, I can ask myself, "Am I prepared to so testify to God's presence in the world as that man did?" *Sh'ma' Yisrael* should be the same way for us, a testimony, a testifying. In the past, people would do that if, *halilah v'has*, they were to be martyred; they would scream out the last *Sh'ma' Yisrael*. And it an ideal to be able to say *Sh'ma' Yisrael* before one takes the last breath.

What is the proper etiquette for going to another house of worship? In the past, I always wanted to let someone there know "I have come because I want to observe your worship; if you wouldn't mind, would you sit next to me and explain to me so that I should understand." Or I would make eye contact someone and say: "Excuse me; I'm here as a guest. Would you please guide me in the service?" Then you can say, "It is my custom that in the presence of God I always wear one of these (pointing to the *kippah*); I hope that won't offend you." I have often made beautiful connections in this way.

151

When I needed to do a silent retreat, I often went to spend time with the Trappist monks of St. Norbert's in Winnipeg or St. Benedict's in Snowmass, Colorado. When the time for prayer came, I would find a place in the back of the chapel where I would stand with my *tallit* and *t'fillin* and *davven* along. When they were saying the Psalms, I would say them in Hebrew while they said them in English or the Latin. There is such a sense of solidarity in this. My God becomes bigger, not smaller, by the fact that I worship side-by-side with another person.

I have also had occasion to be side-by-side with Muslims performing *salat*, saying my own prayers. The big question is always: *Do you understand that I am not meaning to give up my religion as I do this? I'm doing it here like a 'guest,' and I don't want you to think that I am coming here looking for you to be a missionary to me. I want you to know that I come here in a way that wants to honor your place and what you do.* I think that is the proper etiquette.

D'veikut with a Teacher

Much earlier, I discussed the idea of having *d'veikut* with a teacher. The teacher doesn't necessarily have to be alive in this world. If you talk to a Bratzlaver Hasidim* today, they will say, "I'm a Hasid of Rebbe Nahman of Bratzlav." Knowing that he died in 1810, you might ask, "What makes you a Hasid of Rebbe Nahman?" The answer might be: "I try to live my life according to his treachings. I study his works, the *Likkutei MaHaRaN*, and the stories he told. I picture myself in those stories and teachings, and I attune myself to him."

When Catholics used to talk about having a patron saint, what did they have in mind? If you were to read a book by professor Abraham Joshua Heschel, for instance,

---

* Most of them use the pronunciation Breslov today, but the original name was Bratzlav.

and stay with that book for a while, reading it with deep interest, you might ask yourself: "How did it feel to him, what he is describing here? Could I get into that? Could I feel that myself?" In that way, you become a Hasid, as it were, of Heschel at that time. While you are reading him, he is your spiritual ally. You are 'booting' his software, and that takes you to the place you want to go even quicker. It is good to find such spiritual allies, such rebbes in books; you will gain a lot from those apprenticeships.

Shabbat

We have been learning that everything in Torah has four levels of interpretation. There is the simple level that is called *p'shat*. *P'shat* just means 'plain'; there nothing fancy about it. When it says: I give you *Shabbat* "in order that you and your ox and your donkey and your servants can all rest."* Following that, a person might say: "I'm not going to *shul*; I'm not going to do anything but rest on *Shabbat*." Most people have never experienced that. They are always so busy—they have to go to services; they have to do this and that—there is so much to do on *Shabbat*. Sometimes I lie down on the floor on *Shabbat*, I stretch out and let go of every one of my muscles. I breathe in and I breathe out, and then I let go of the leg muscles, the shoulder muscles, and so on. Then I have a sense of really being carried by the ground. That is also doing *Shabbat*. I've done *Shabbat* in *p'shat*. Obviously there are higher levels of *Shabbat*, even in the *pshat* level.

If I go to the level of *remez*, I realize that *Shabbat* is not just a certain amount of time—24 or 26 hours—it is a kind of *being*. It is that which says: "I need not to strive; everything is as it should be." Do you remember the Max Ehrmann poem called "Desiderata"? That was such a wonderful *Shabbesdik* poem: "You are a child of the universe, no less than the trees and the stars; you have a

---

* Exodus 23:12.

153

right to be here." You don't have to strive for anything; whatever you need is already in you. All is right with the world. In *remez*, the *Shabbat* is not only in your body, but also in a feeling place.

I used to live in Winnipeg, Canada, and sometimes with the wind chill factor, it was about 70 degrees below zero. I would come home from *shul* on Friday night wearing a fur-lined coat and my mustache and my beard had icicles on them. I'd come into the house and say, "Good *Shabbes!*" There was a kind of thawing out: *I'm finally home. The smells are wonderful and now I can relax. I'm in* Shabbes. I like saying "Good *Shabbes!*" more than, "*Shabbat shalom, Shabbat shalom, Shabbat shalom.*" I feel this is like a train going with that clipped rhythm. I like the expansiveness of "Good *Shabbes!*"

With the level of *d'rash*, we come to the mind of *Shabbat*. It sees the perfection of things. If you were to ask Moshe *rabbeinu* how he felt as the leader of the Israelites, I can't imagine that he would say, "I had such a good time." Nevertheless, we say, *Yismah Moshe*, "Moshe is happy with the gift that God gave him."* *Ha'Shem* made him the mediator of *Shabbat* for us. Then you begin to think about what it means to be productive; what does it mean to enjoy what there is? You look at the difference between how the world is during the weekdays, and you recognize what it could be beyond—*b'yom sh'kullo Shabbat*—if everything in the world would be harmonious and organic. Then you go into the vision of *Shabbat,* and that is the next level.

Every phase of *Shabbat* has a different texture. The Zohar tells us that Friday night is called *Hakal Tappuhin kaddishin*, a sacred apple orchard. What is the apple orchard? On Friday afternoon, before *Shabbat,* we recite the Song of Songs. There it says that the lover reminds the beloved saying, It was underneath the apple tree that I

---

* This is said on *Shabbat.*

stimulated you, my beloved.* That's a marvelous romantic picture, but it also says that that is the time for the *Shekhinah*, the Shabbat Queen. Do you get all that? *Shabbat*, at that point, is really feminine, and you celebrate coming home to mother. Even though the *Shulhan Arukh* says that the *seuda* of *Shabbat* noon should be fancier, it never is. Friday night is always fancier because it is closer to the cooking. You are coming home to mother's cooking. How does mother show you love? *Eat, my child; eat, eat. A whole week you were deprived; now I want to take away all tht deprivation. I really want you to be at home. Eat; enjoy, enjoy, enjoy.*

If I start looking at the universe like my mother, at nature like my mother, I'm buoyed up; I'm given oxygen to breathe and food to eat. Gravity is holding me up. I celebrate all these things. That is part of the flavor of Friday night, which also includes the Zohar's teaching that it is the night for lovers, because that is the time when God and the *Shekhinah* also come together.

Friday night is linked to the generosity of father Abraham. *Shabbat* morning is not Abraham, but Isaac, and that takes you up to such a high place, where Isaac is on the altar. In Kabbalah, it is called the "ancient of days." That is very mental, and that's the reason why people read, study, and talk Torah. *Shabbat* morning doesn't have the same visceral feel as Friday night. Do you see what I mean by that texture of things?

Shabbat afternoon for *ShaleShuedes — S'udah shlishit* is different. If you have ever attended a good *ShaleShuedes*, you have seen the difference — the melodies, the setting sun, no artificial light. You sit with a group as *Shabbat* is waning and sing, and then you hear a little Torah and reflect on it. Then you sit in silence. You sing *Z'miros*. *Shabbat* goes away slowly, slowly, slowly.

---

* Song of Solomon 2:1-7.

Most American Jews have only had Friday night, and to them, that is when it is good.

In Jewish Renewal, there is *davvenen* with a lot of happiness and dancing; but in most *shuls* in the past, that was not what was happening. Nevertheless, if you were there, and there was no *bar-mitzvah*, you were there to *davven*. You had a certain routine to follow and it made you feel good to do it; this is also a good model.

The attitude that comes through on *Shabbat* morning, with its longer *davvenen* and Torah reading, is part of a different phase of *Shabbat*. There's a different flavor to it, and you may have to go in search of that flavor today. But even if you have experienced Friday night *Shabbat* and *Shabbat* morning, not many today have experienced *ShaleSheudas*. This is the third phase of *Shabbat*, in which you sit together and ask, "Where will I take the energy, spiritual nourishment that I will need for the week?" *ShaleSheudas* is where you draw it in. It is like the *Neilah*. Yom Kippur is going away, and you want to know if you have you achieved it. Have you been forgiven? It is a strong time, and it is important that people should know that.

There is another phase that mostly is overlooked to-day, called *Melave Malka,* escorting the Queen out after *Shabbat* is over. This was a time when people would take out their fiddles and play, and they would sing *niggunim*. When I was in Winnipeg, that was a time when they cooked potatoes and herring and put out schnapps, and ocassionally beer. People would come to celebrate. It was like "Everyone Loves Saturday Night."* It had that feel-ing. It's called "The Meal of King David." That's when there would be poetry and all kinds of wonderful things. Most importantly, stories would be told at that time. They say, if you tell a story of the Ba'al Shem Tov on Sat-urday evening, after *Havdalah,* you are guaranteed to make a living that week.

---

* A popular song by Kenny Chandler.

So, you should have all the *brokhes*. I wish you to be able to dance. I wish you to be able to visit worshipers of other kinds, so that you will be just jealous enough of how they do it, so that you will be moved to improve your own worship, and to do it with greater commitment. And don't forget to talk to God in the vernacular. All the blessings. *Kol tuv* — Amen.

Question and Answer Session

Question: Going back to dancing with prayer, do you have a vision of how you could dance with other people? Just as we *davven* in a *minyan*, could we dance in a *minyan*?

Reb Zalman: In Fort Collins, Colorado, there used to be a congregation of people who were 'affiliates' to Judaism, though they were not born Jewish and had not undergone conversion as you would expect. Their leader had followed Shlomo Carlebach around for a couple years and had brought back melodies for them. They called themselves *Adat Elohim*, the congregation of God, and they wore outfits for services that were like Shlomo's: men in *kippot*, white shirts and black vests, while the women wore nice skirts and blouses, and some of them wore kerchiefs over their hair. And they did such beautiful dances to Shlomo's melodies. They had a band that would play, and they would do that in the middle of the week, and I would come up from time to time to be with them.

Now, the problem of getting a dance *minyan* together would be great in some other city, but in Boulder should be a real possibility. There's enough music here, and there are enough people who know about the body. But you have to watch out; you don't want it to be like Israeli folk dancing, like the *hora*. You would have to begin with learning body movement.

I used to do that with students. I would have them lie down on the floor. I would put on "The Art of the Fugue" by Bach and then I would say, "When you hear the first voice, use the right arm to dance to that. When you hear the second voice, use the left arm to dance to that while the right continues." Before long, they had all four voices, and they were moving the arms and the legs at the same time.

Before I even start that, I would have them stand in a circle and we would play the "Hokey-Pokey," so we 'put the whole of self in.' Later on, after we graduated to letting the body go in the music, rather than imposing movement on it, we got to the place where people were able to dance a minuet with God. The music was the Rolling Stones' "19th Nervous Breakdown," which was like Rolling Stones baroque. It is a very beautiful piece that allows you to do this kind of dance with God. We did this all with lights down, because it wasn't to impress others. When you do that kind of a dance, you really have to stay inside of yourself with it, and others can do the same.

To get to the place where you can dance as a pair, and still do this with the right *kavvanah*, takes some work. But I think it is wonderful. You have reciprocal group dances — this group comes together and goes apart, then the other one comes in — there are so many ways to do it. Reb Elimelekh of Lizhensk had such a dance.* These are the dances that are meant to get you out of the head. After a while, you would see people dance in such a way that they would get ecstatic in it and still dance as a group. Chabad people have a way of dancing as a wheel. They make a wheel, put arms into the center and then they stomp around the circle. That is a very powerful kind of energizing the field, but I have also seen more aesthetic ways of dancing.

---

* Rabbi Elimelekh of Lizhensk (1717-1786), the founder of Polish Hasidism.

Comment: I wonder if you could speak a bit more about when God doesn't answer your prayer.

Reb Zalman: Part of the answer has to do with 'hanging up the phone too soon,' as I mentioned earlier. Another part has to do with a story of a little girl who prayed to God for a particular doll, and didn't get it. They said to her, "You see, God didn't listen to your prayer." She said: "That is not true; God listened, but He said 'No.'" When you have a sense that the universe is saying, "In this formulation, what you're asking is not going to be best for the whole," it is easier to understand. Then the question becomes, "So in which way should I ask?" Sometimes you have the wrong address for someone, and the message doesn't get there.

I'm not going to say that you are always going to get the desired response, even if you have the right address, and ask the right question. Sometimes you will feel abandoned.

In Psalm 22:2, it says, *"Eli, Eli lamah 'azavtani,* "My God, my God, why have You forsaken me?" It is a heavy thing to feel that way. Or think of what Jeremiah 20:7 says, "You seducer, God," You dragged me into this; You really twisted my head. It is interesting that he has the *hutzpah* to say 'You have seduced me, God; this wasn't right.' But consider how real God has to be to him in order to say that.

Reb Michael, did you have something you wanted to relate?

Reb Michael: A few months ago you said that we have holes in our consciousness, but there are also distortions where we don't have holes.

Reb Zalman: We were talking then about the 'flaw.' The flaw is something like a contaminant in us that doesn't allow us to go straight, something that twists. Every time we make a mistake, it seems to be another version of the same mistake. You can battle this for a long, long time, but everyone has a flaw. If we were all perfect, God's world would lack differentiation.

The flaw is a very important. You can think of it like a missing puzzle piece; without it, the puzzle is never going to be right. That is one way in which the flaw manifests sometimes. But sometimes it also manifests in such a way that it skews your view of reality.

Right now, I am dealing with macular degeneration in one eye. In the early phases of it, they would show me a grid, and if I could see all the lines straight, it was good; but when I focused on the center, I would see that the center was sort of twisted. The lines were not straight. That was a sign that something was happening on my retina, that I wasn't seeing well.

If I were try and measure people's moral sense, I would find that almost everyone has a little bit macular degeneration there; that it's not quite straight. Then the question is: How do we deal with that? That's why I think 'socialized meditation' is so important; because unless we have friends with whom we can really talk, from whom we don't have to hide, we won't be able to socialize our spirituality.

If I have to present myself as always being perfect, then I'm going to prove to be such a hypocrite. I need to have someone with whom I can level. Before every Rosh Hashanah, I have a conversation with three of my friends, whom I ask: "What did you see in me this year that you think I need to shift?" Of what distortions might I unaware? In Psalm 19:13-15 it says: "Who knows his own error? From the hidden things, clean me up. Then can I become whole, complete; I will be cleansed from great sin." Then it says: "Please accept my prayer and the meditation of my heart, my rock and my Redeemer." These are two *p'sukim* (verses) that can benefit us greatly.

Tenth Talk
Elements of Davvenenology

In India, you have raga singers who will sing 'morning ragas' and 'evening ragas' with modes varying according to the time. That is to say, time has quality, and there are different modes for different times.

On *Shabbat*, it is said that we have an additional soul; we have a *neshamah y'terah.*. This is not like getting an extra piece of *gefilte* fish, that you have soul and then you get another *shtikle* soul. It means is that on *Shabbat* your soul occupies a higher region. You are more *neshomadik*—*neshama y'terah*—you've gone to a higher vibratory place with it. On that level, there is more confluence, more oneness.

People used say, "Every clock that is stopped is right twice a day." What are those two times for the highest sensitivity of prayer? Are they the places where the day and nighttime consciousness meet at the dawn and dusk?

Sometimes I feel sad coming into a *shul* at ten o'clock in the morning and hearing them say, "You give the rooster understanding the difference between day and night."ha* It is, *nebbukh*, a confused rooster who first starts crowing at ten o'clock. When you read the *dinim*, the laws about it, it is very clear that the important thing is to be there *b'netz ha'hamah*, when the sun comes over the horizon. For this reason, I used to take the kids at various summer camps up on a mountain facing east to pray and watch the sunrise. From time to time, when the weather permits, I also go up to the ridge at NCAR overlooking Boulder Valley or to Flagstaff to watch and pray

---

* *Birkhot Ha'Shahar* in the morning liturgy.

with the sunrise. These are beautiful high places where you can look out and you see the sunrise all over the city and the prairie land, and it seems like a miracle. You are right there when it happens, witnessing the mingling of night and day, the coming together of romantic time and practical time. That's a good mingling.

It is the same situation on Highway 1, when you go down from San Francisco to Los Angeles. At sunset, see how many cars have stopped on the side of the road just to watch it. As the sun sinks and sinks and sinks, and you reflect on it, you realize that when the sun is rising, we are falling toward the sun. Or when the sun is setting, you are falling away from the sun. These are the kinds of things you don't think unless you are actually there at that time.

Working with the Siddur

Susan: I'm interested in this idea of how we can take the restocking of our experience in morning prayer more seriously; I'm having trouble imagining how to do that.

Reb Zalman: The people who helped to form the *siddur* were serious people. Standing in the presence of God and expressing themselves in this way was their business. On the other hand, their life experiences were not quite like ours. The *siddur* contains a history of our people, but not everything in it speaks to our life experiences in the present. Some things in the *siddur* speak to me when I am elated, and some when I'm in need of help. Sometimes I ask, "What do I need to have for this particular day?" When you do this, this already says that you are taking your *davvenen* more seriously, because you want it to achieve something, to answer to your prayer, to help you get through your day in the right way. This is why you want to look and see which parts of the *davvenen* are most helpful to that end and highlight them. If you can do this before the *davvenen,* you will be better off; it will go smoother, because you will have planned the way ahead.

Sometimes you may get derailed. Sometimes this is because you didn't know what you needed to pray for, and all of a sudden, something else shows itself as being more needful. Then I would say, "follow that," because that is a minor form of prophecy.

Again, all of this becomes real for us when we connect it with our practical reality.

There was a great *rebbe,* Kalonymus Kalmish of Piasetzno, who said that people talk about the secret and the revealed teaching. They say all the laws of *Shabbat* and kosher and so on are revealed teaching, and the things having to do with Kabbalah are hidden teaching. But so many books have been printed about Kabbalah that there are no more hidden teachings. So what is still hidden and secret? The Piasetzner says that the secret is in the experience of God, in the moment when you are feeling that God is really in and with you. In that little moment, you are 'logged-on,' and that's the secret. Even if I asked you to tell me about it, you couldn't so adequately. Also, you don't want to get into boasting and ego-inflation. There are moments in *davvenen* when you feel: "Yes, it is for real. This is for real." That's a secret in *davvenen.*

Many translators and editors of the *siddur* over the years were doing left-brain translation and redaction. But prayer comes more from the heart through the right brain and is better understood in terms of poetry. When you look at the Hebrew in *P'sukei d'Zimrah,* you find an interesting thing. *Ashrei yoshvei veytekha, od y'halelukha selah.** You find that you have a half a sentence and then the other half of the sentence sort of repeats part of it and

---

* "Praisworthy are those who dwell in your house; may they always praise You!"

163

nails it down. That is called in Hebrew 'the doubling of the language,' *kefel ha'lashon.* That is our kind of poetry.

In *Ashrei,* we say: *Pote'ah et yadekha u'mashbia' l'khol hai ratzon,* "You open Your hand and You satisfy us with everything that we want and need." Immediately, you see we are dealing with imagery, metaphor, and poetry. If the right brain were not functioning, the left brain would say: "This is nonsense. God doesn't have a hand that puts food in my belly. What are you *hakin a tchainik?** What are you going on about?" That is the left brain. For the right brain it is not a problem. *Pote'ah et yadekha u'mashbia' l'khol hai ratzon.*

The issue of *davvenen* is so misunderstood because the people who translated the *siddur* did a left brain translation, as if they were saying, "Look, I'm giving you a left-brain translation so you should be able to learn what the Hebrew means." I used to get to a line when I was leading congregational services out of the Birnbaum prayer book that still makes me laugh: "Thou hast exalted my horn like a wild ox." It is a good literal translation of *vatarem kiR'eym karniy baloti bashemen ra'anan,* "You have anointed my head with oil." But obviously, this translation does not translate what the author, who was a poet, had in mind. So how should I translate it? "You have given me energy and hope. You have raised my sights, God. I feel so juicy inside because of that." That is a good figurative translation of *vatarem kiR'eym karniy.* When we understand that *davvenen* is not a left brain function, we begin to get that the words do not have to be taken literally. Very few people have come to terms with that.

Some years ago, I went and recorded the *davvenen* in a studio. I recorded one track in English for the right ear, going to the left brain, and one track in Hebrew for the left ear, going to the right brain. And you listen to them simultaneously, beginning to put the English and the Hebrew together.

---

* Yiddish, literally 'knocking a teakettle.'

I don't know if you've ever seen this beautiful picture of an Orthodox *frum* woman with her hair covered. She's holding on to the strap in the subway and in the other hand she holds little *siddur*. It is a beautiful picture. What I had in mind is that, when you are really in a rush, you could play this recording in the car and *davven* along with it.

Niggunim and the Right Brain

What language does the right brain like? The language of *niggunim*, melodies.

This is just a side issue, but I want to bring it in. Many people who convert to Judaism go to classes where they are taught all the left brain information about Judaism: "This is what we believe. These are the holy days. These are the laws. This is what you have to do." Very seldom do people get an aesthetic, right brain education in Judaism. You could almost learn somatically how to talk like a Jew, with your whole body: "All my bones speak it."*

Lenny Bruce used to talk about "Jewish and goyish." White bread and green Jell-O were goyish. Very few people who come into Judaism get into that part which is in the body and the right brain to feel that. I've been saying to people who are on the way to convert: "Play a lot of Jewish music in the house. Get to feel it." A generation ago, if I were to begin to sing a certain Yiddish lullaby, people would start crying right away. *Rozinkes mit Mandlen* was the name of the song in Yiddish. It was nostalgic for them. It is like the tail of a kite. It won't fly unless you have a little bit of that nostalgia for the days gone. So music has a very important part to play in our right brain education.

Shlomo Carlebach was an absolute genius with this, because he was able to take from the older European mode and update it with a rhythm and harmony that

---

* Psalms 35:10.

165

somehow made it American. It was a good transition that he created for us.

Some *niggunim* are very serious, like the *niggun* of Reb Mikheleh of Zlotchov that the Ba'al Shem Tov wanted to have sung when we needed him to pray with us. Gurdjieff used to say that there are some melodies that are fluff, and some that he called "objective music."* I once heard a piece that Gurdjieff played on the harmonium and it sounded very much like some of the Lubavitcher *niggunim*. It had that same feel, a certain somberness and longing. There are pieces of music that do that. I would like, for instance, to suggest to you that you do something that I once did. Once I went through all the piano concertos of Mozart and took out the lentos (slow parts) and recorded them one after another. Can you imagine how lovely the music would be? They all have that wonderful feeling.

Sometimes I have a sense that it is important to offer 'God music.' How to do that? Just two or three years before the wall came down, I was in Poland. We were doing a series of teachings in Krakow, and at the finale, Mozart's great and solemn mass was to be performed by the Polish Radio Orchestra. They asked me to introduce this is as a prayer. How could we hear this prayerfully? I said that the best thing that you can do is close your eyes, open your heart, feel the music, float with the music, and say, "Dear God, this exquisite feeling that this music produces in me, I offer up to You." Sometimes this is a lot better than words. If you have the right pieces of music, let them do this for you.

Sometimes my kids ask me to be more open to modern music, but I am afraid I got stuck with the Beatles and the Moody Blues—I didn't make it much past that. I can go back to stuff like George Harrison's "My Sweet Lord" and *davven* in a happy way with that, but the gap has

---

* George Ivanovich Gurdjieff (ca. 1866-1949), Armenian born spiritual teacher.

generally become too large for me. Nevertheless, these connections are still important to make for yourselves.

God's Corner

It is important to create a "God's corner" in your house. There is a Hasidic tale about a *rebbe* in the forest with his Hasidim. When it was time to *davven Minhah,* he was attracted to *davven* at a particular tree. Later he found that some fifty years before, another *tzaddik* had davvened at that tree, and it is still had that vibe and it attracted him. There is something about making a *makom kavu'a* for your prayer. It doesn't have to be a lot of space — one corner with a little table on which you can put your candles and you keep your *tallit* and *t'fillin* is enough. That's where you do your *davvenen,* so that the space entrains you also.

Whenever possible, light candles. It is the last sacrifice we have. We don't have any others. We don't need the light; we have other lights to read by. What's left is that we are offering the candle. We are saying, "Dear God, 'the soul of a human being is a candle of the Lord,' and I want to light it." It is like the Doors' song "Light My Fire." So we say, "Come on, God, light my fire," and you light those candles. It makes a difference in the *davvenen.*

Making Your Own Tools

When I was teaching at Camp Ramah, I would have the kids make their own *tallitot.* I went to different manufacturers for remnants and got them together. I got a sewing machine and showed them how to do it. The kids came in and they made their own *tallitot*: different colors, different stripes, whatever they wanted to make. It makes such a difference to have a *tallit* that you made yourself.

What are the dimensions? It should be from fingers of one outstretched arm to another. It should be from the top of the head to the knees, at least. That is the width. You get a piece of cloth that you like and hem it in the way that you want. Sew on the four corners into which the *tzitzit* are going to be tied. There are some very beautiful things in fabric stores with which you can embellish it: inch-wide ribbon in different colors. You can sew them on and make a beautiful *tallit* that you've invested your own time and effort in. It's not just a give away.

With the *t'fillin*, it is much harder. It would take far too much to make your own, if it were even possible. But a *mezuzzah* is possible. I used to have the kids at the camp write the *Sh'ma'* on a 3 x 5 card: the *Sh'ma'* and *v'haya im-sha'mo'a*, and then shape a container for their own door. Halakhically, this is not quite kosher; but what does it say in Torah? "And you shall write them upon the door posts of your house and your gates." I told them, "Use this *mezuzzah* for your bedroom, the room that is *your* room in the house. If you have a hard time falling asleep, then pay attention when you write *b'shokhb'kha*, 'when you lie down.' If you have a hard time getting up, pay attention when you write *u'vkumekha*, 'when you get up.'"* You can you put your own *kavvanah* in the *mezuzzah* you make. What a difference it makes if we put our own energy into it.

When Time is Short

What do we do when time is short? If we can, we should put on *tallit* and *t'fillin* and say the *Sh'ma'* and leave the rest of it for later, for better situations. It would be nice if you can do it in order. But some people eat dessert before they eat the meal. What can I say? It may not be the ideal way to do it, but at least it is done.

When I look at my appointment calendar, I'm not happy about it, because it is blocked in hours and often my appointments are right next to one another. I would

---

* Deuteronomy 6:9,7.

like to have at least seven minutes between appointments to sit down, let go of the previous appointment, and make a little connection 'Upstairs': "Thank you, God, for being with me and helping me to make a switch so that I can really be with the next person, and not be continuing to speak to the situation of the last person." On the one hand, it seems so obvious to do that; but on the other, we usually don't. It really very helpful, and I can witness to that.

Situational Thinking

Most spiritual and religious discourse is very abstract. People love to talk about the infinite, about how 'beyond' God is, and it is always left brain stuff. It has very little to do with my own personal situation vis-à-vis God. In Hasidic language, that is called *ada'ata d'nafshey*, which Heschel called "situational thinking." You're not merely thinking about something separate and abstract from you; *you are in the situation.* I call this 'participatory epistemology.' We are used to thinking of something, and asking: "Do I understand it?" It is very distant from us, and we don't think that we participate in it. But the Heisenberg uncertainty principle tells us that we cannot speak about anything without taking the observer into consideration. We have to start thinking, "I'm in the picture." When I think about *yeztiyat mitzrayim* and the giving of the Torah, and I think in the abstract, then I'm not in the picture. It has to be *ada'ata d'nafshey*, situational thinking.

I often use an example about a doctor friend of yours who invites you to look in his microscope. He says: "I want to show you something. This is a healthy cell and this is a cancerous cell. See how I stained it? Can you see the difference?" You say, "Yes, that's very interesting." "Well," he says, "do you remember the biopsy I took of you the other day?" What happens? It is not abstract anymore. Your stomach lurches. That's *ada'ata d'nafshey*.

Using All Four Levels

When I want to learn *Gemara* or learn a *din*, I want to focus very narrowly. But when I'm *davvenen*, I want to open the aperture. I want to know that the word that I am saying has meaning on ascending levels. For this reason, when you study Torah, they tell you there is *P'shat*, *Remez*, *D'rash*, and *Sod*. They are the four levels of interpretation: the simple meaning, the deductive meaning, the inductive meaning, and the secret meaning.

In order to help people see this, in *Paradigm Shift* I once wrote a symphonic notation of the *Amidah*. If you have ever seen the score that the conductor of a symphony uses, he has so many lines for just a short piece of music, because there are the violins, cellos, woodwinds, etc. — and he's got it all in front of him.

If someone really wants to get into *davvenen*, it is important to investigate all the levels: *What do I do with my body? Where do I put my feelings? On what level am I doing my thinking? And in which way am I going to try to merge with God?* What does the word *barukh* mean in the separate worlds of action, feeling, thinking, and being? Do you see what I'm saying? That calls for an almost symphonic awareness in *davvenen*, and I don't think this is something that you will be able to do immediately. You have to add elements gradually, trying to bring more and more into the awareness of the *davvenen*. If you were to ask what would go on in the mind of someone who is fully aware of all those things in the *davvenen*, it would be beyond my understanding; but I want to stretch into that direction, as if I could feel it.

The Bedtime Sh'ma'

I want to talk about the bedtime *Sh'ma'* before we go to sleep. It is good to study this in the *siddur* and to see how it says there the prayer for forgiveness: "I forgive anyone who has hurt or angered me, in this incarnation or any other, and let no one be punished on my account."

That is very important, very necessary. Then there is a prayer: "Grant that we should have a quiet night; that we should lie down in peace." Always keep in mind: "*Ribbono shel Olam*, may it be a boring night for the police, for the firefighters, and for the ambulance drivers, because for people who work with emergencies, a 'good night' is quiet." Keep that in mind also as you say these prayers. Revisit the day and note the places where you can say, "That was good; for this I give thanks." Or, "That needs fixing" and "I forgot to do this." So at the end of the day, you cash in, as it were, on your actions. All of that goes with the bedtime *Sh'ma'*.

Contributing to the Energy Bank

The 'energy bank' created by the religious community is very important for doing spiritual work. Do you remember how it was when President Obama was inaugurated? The energy of hope was so thick that, if it could have been translated into dollars, we could have paid off the national debt then and there. People created that energy.

Now, often when Jews have to draw God-credit from the universal bank, we often get a message that says, 'insufficient funds.' I don't know if that make sense to you, but I want to spell it out. With every *mitzvah* that I do, with every prayer that I make, I enlarge the space in which God can dwell. That is what the Kotzker Rebbe was saying when he asked, "Where is God?" But instead of saying, "Everywhere," he said, "Wherever we let Him in."[*] *B'libbi mishkan evneh*, "In my heart I will build a sanctuary."[**] That God-space, which you create with your prayer, is filled with energy as you create it.

---

[*] Rabbi Menachem Mendel Morgenstern of Kotzk (1787-1859), a *rebbe* of the Pyshyskha school of Hasidism.

[**] From a poem by Rabbi Eliezer Azikri (1533-1600).

If I had to draw on that energy for healing, it would be so important to be able to have access to the account of Jewish spiritual capital. Most people don't pay attention to that; they are always thinking that God has enough, and that God can do anything, especially when it is convenient to do so. But we have a relationship with God, a partnership. And when we keep out end, the account is replenished.

During the High Holy Days, in the middle of *davvenen*, you sometimes get a sense that you are surrounded by spiritual energy, because people are investing energy there. The pool of energy in the religious community is charged; the reservoir is filled.

That's an important thing to remember on days when you don't feel much like *davvenen*; the energy pool needs you to *davven*.

They used to make a joke about the people in Chelm. Wondering how they were going to pay their rabbi his salary, they came up with the following plan: everyday, each member of the community would bring a little glass of schnapps and pour it into a barrel, and at the end of the year, they would sell the barrel of schnapps to earn the rabbi's salary. Well, the end of the year came and they opened the barrel to taste the schnapps, and found that it was all water. You see, everyone figured that the others were adding schnapps and thus, they could add little glass of water without anyone else noticing.

If I were to ask where the Jewish barrel at this point, I would say that it is more water than schnapps.

Faith-ing

Now let's talk about faith for a moment. I don't like to talk about "having faith." In Judaism, faith is something you do, it is verb. When I'm *faith-ing*, then it's real. When I stop *faith-ing*, then there is no faith; it doesn't exist. Its existence is only there in my actually doing it. The matrix of everything that I have discussed in these talks is the faith with which says, "I want to be loyal to the purpose that created me." That's faith, *emunah*, in the sense that I want to be loyal to the purpose that created me.

At the moment I start praying, placing myself in the presence of God, I don't have litmus paper to prove that God is present; all I have is an affirmation: *I affirm that I am standing in the presence of God. I affirm that this is for real for me. I faith that.* You take that away, and the whole matrix collapses. I have a sense that God cares about what I do, that God creates me, and my life is significant. I have no proof of that, but I am faith-ing it.

Sometimes I like to use the word 'be-live' instead of 'believe.' That is to say, I invest in something because of my experience with it. When I get up from this chair, I will *be-living* in gravity. Faith is something like that. It is not an idea that I hold, but I do live on the basis that it is for real. This is when someone usually asks: "But how do you know this is real? How do you know this is not something that you have made up in your mind?" While I may be able to come up with a bunch of reasons, I don't want to do that; the purity of faith-ing must say, "I don't have any proof of this, but my intuition says 'Yes' to it." Faith is something that goes with the level of intuition.

How do I know something in intuition? Because *I am that*; it's not that I know something objectively, outside of me. I know it because I am that; I am in that. I place myself in that place. That's what I'm talking about with *emunah*, faith.

I want to wish all of you, when next you are tempted to say, "Come on, I'm only making it up for myself," that you be given a moment in which the Divine Presence will reveal its secret in your awareness. From that, you will be sustained in so many things in your life.

Lighting the Candles on Shabbat

One last thing about lighting candles on Friday night. Sometimes I wish that I could pray during the week, a whole week, with the same fervor, sincerity, and power that my mother had when she stood before the candles and prayed on *Shabbat* for every one of her children and grandchildren and great-grandchildren. All of them were on her list, and she had something to pray for them from God. Then she went larger and larger and larger. It was a very special time.

The good part of the candle lighting prayer is that you don't have a formula other than making the blessing: *Barukh ata Ha'Shem asher kidyshanu b'mitzvotav vitzivanu l'hadlik ner shel Shabbat Kodesh.* She would say the formula, but then she stood in front of the candles and continued to pray. I think the more we can make these prayers, the deeper our experience of *Shabbat* is going tobe. If you are single and you light your own candles, then you can do this. If you are with your partner and they are saying the prayer, then you can say, "I support you in your prayer, and offer my energy to it."

It used to be the custom to put *tzedakah,* some charity money into the *pushke,* the charity box, for the week that had passed before lighting the candles on Friday night. This was an important custom, and should be renewed.

Question and Answer Session

Question: In the beginning, you talked about dusk and dawn as minor and major modes. Well, I struggle with major prayers, happy prayers, like the *halleluyah.* I really relate more to *Sh'ma' kolenu,* I'm in pain. I don't always feel, "Oh, the world is beautiful." I'm just feeling my pain and my selfishness, or whatever it is.

Reb Zalman: You know, from time to time, I'm asked to do something in a public prayer situation. The last time I was in Aspen, there was a meeting of people from different religions and they asked me to lead them in a prayer. So I asked the people to stand up, and I began to chant directions to them: *"When I chant this line, you respond . . . Ha-le-lu-yah."* Then I began to chant one line after another, and each time I completed a line, the people responded, *"Ha-le-lu-yah."* I asked them to harmonize and really get into it. By the time I had been through the whole list of things to bless and be grateful for, the people were so high. There were even a couple of African American ladies there who got it on their own wavelength in such a wonderful way that it took them a while to cool down!

That's a high point, but there are other times when it isn't necessarily such an explosion, times that are also happy because we are speaking to God, but which do not seem happy. I think this is a great antidote to the *kvetch.* In our tradition, we say: *Mish'nikhnas Adar marbin b'simhah,* "When Adar comes, you increase joy." And the Kotzker Rebbe added, *Mish'nikhnas Av m'ma'atin b'simhah,* "When the month of Av comes" — when we mourn the destruction of the Temple — "we do less joy." There is less *simhah,* but there is always *simhah.* I think that's a good thing to remember.

Eleventh Talk
Preperation for Davvenen

Today is the *yahrzeit* of Moshe *rabbeinu*, and it's also the *yahrzeit* of Reb Eisig Kalover.* First I want to say something about Moshe *rabbeinu*, because we wouldn't be talking about any of this had he not been who he was. In the Orthodox world, most people see Moshe *rabbeinu* as a great and learned *ga'on*, almost as if he had studied in some kind of Orthodox *yeshivah*. But if we take the story in the *Humash* seriously, and we should, then it is clear that he probably got the best Egyptian education that anyone could in his day. As a princeling of Pharoah's house, he would likely have gone to the Harvard of his time. In the movie, *The Ten Commandments*, we see that he and Rameses, the future Pharoah, are really peers and competing princes.

But then something happens to him when he sees the suffering of his people. I tell you, this is this something that happens to every Jew, no matter how assimilated. When we encounter anti-Semitism, something is aroused in us, just as it was in Theodor Herzl. When he went to Paris as a reporter to cover the infamous Dreyfus trial for the *Neue Freie Presse,* which in those days was like the *New York Times* of Europe, he was an assimilated German Jew. But as he walked through the streets of Paris, witnessing this farcical trial, someone yelled out him, *Sal Juif,* "Dirty Jew!" When you start thinking that the result of that experience was Zionism, you begin to wonder what Moshe *rabbeinu* must have felt as an assimilated Egyptian Hebrew, only his reaction resulted in Judaism!

---

* Rabbi Yitzhak Eisig of Kalov (1751-1821), a disciple of the MAggid of Mezritch.

Something very powerful had happened to him and he couldn't stay in Egypt because he is a wanted man.

Where does he go? Into the desert. Later we find him with the shaman of the desert, Yitro, the *kohen* of Midian. What does it mean to be a priest for the wandering Bedouins? You are both prophet and healer. And Moshe was his apprentice.

Then we come to the burning bush and his encounter with God. We see him at this point in Psalm 90:1-2, when he says, "From generation to generation, You have been our God, before the mountains were created."

And by the end of his life, he has tried to lead us out of the dark, but the Korachs among the people have hindered him. So I just want to say: "Moshe *rabbeinu,* I thank you for having lived. I thank you for having been the conduit of Torah for us."

When Moshe *rabbeinu* was in heaven, about to receive the Torah, he heard someone teaching Torah, and he could not comprehend what was being said. So he asks God, "What's going on here?" And God says, "Have a little patience." It was Rabbi Akiva holding forth. And soon someone asked him, "Where do you get this teaching from?" He answers, *Halakhah l'Moshe mi-Sinai,* "I got it from Moses who received it at Sinai." Then Moshe feels better.

So I want to say, "Dear Moshe *rabbeinu,* even if it seems strange to you, I tell you that we got it all from you."

Now I want to go to Reb Eisig, the Kalover Rebbe, who as a child made his living as a goose-herd in Hungary, where geese were a staple of food.

One day, one of the hidden *tzaddikim,* Reb Leib Sarah's comes along, and talks to Reb Eisig, who is just a boy at the time. He sees that the child has a great light burning in him, and so he goes to the child's mother and says to her: "What's the use having of this child raising geese? Let me take him with me, and I will bring him to a good *yeshivah*. I know that you are a poor widow and you need the little money he brings in, so here is some money to take care of your needs."

So she gives him permission to take little Eisig, and he delivers him to the *yeshivah* of Reb Shmelke of Nikolsburg, and in time, he becomes a great *tzaddik*.

I like that he spoke Hungarian, and felt it was necessary to do things in the vernacular. He even conducted a whole *seder* in Hungarian, which upset some people. There is also a well-known story of how he once heard a gypsy playing music in a tavern and said to him, "Will you sell me this song?" The gypsy thought this was a ridiculous thing to ask; but Reb Eisig told him, "I want to be able to pay you for something so valuable." So the gypsy taught him the song.

In English translation, the original words go something like this: "It's the morning and the cock is crowing, and I'm becoming aware of how lonely I am. There is a bird before me, and I say, 'Bird, will you do me a favor? When you fly across the forest, will you greet my beloved and tell her, when the winter is over, I'll marry up with her.'"

But the Kalover saw this as the relationship between us and God and made the words: "Bird, bird, where are you flying?" "South—it's getting colder; I'm flying to *Yerushalayim*." "Would you do me a favor? When you get to the *Kotel*, tell the *Shekhinah*, when the *golus* (exile) is over, I'll come right away."

In Yiddish, the last stanza says: "When will this be? When the Temple will be rebuilt and Zion will be filled with people, then it will be."

So I'm asking also you—like Reb Eisig Kalover, who understood why it was necessary to teach in the vernacular—to *davven* in the vernacular.

Intentions and Distractions

Now I want to talk about basic preparation for *davvenen,* because I am coming to the end of this series of talks. I know I have repeated many things, and will repeat them again, but this is necessary if what I want to say is going to sink in.

First of all, it is always necessary to say before *davvenen:* "This is what I intend to do." If you look in the old *siddurim* (and even some not-so-old *siddurim*) you will find the words: *Hineni Mukhan um'zumman,* "I am ready." *That is to say:* "I feel myself invited to do this *davvenen,* and so I'm stepping in to it willingly. I want to tell you my personal motivations for *davvenen.* The first is *l'shem yihud kudesha brikhu u'sh'khintei,* for the sake of bringing about the union of God transcendent with God immanent, right here and now. Another is to connect myself to all of Israel, to remove the barriers between me and others that I may have created. I want to love every person of Israel like myself, and plug into all sentient beings in my *davvenen.* I know is that my particular *davvenen,* no matter how good it is, will be just one little tile in the mosaic of all humanity praying to God. I know that I can't do it alone, and thus I say, *B'shem kol Yisrael,* I want to be included with everyone else. I remove any hatred from my heart and wish to love everyone in my prayer. On that basis, I say *hineni Mukhan um'zumman,* now I am ready to pray."

Once, my *rebbe,* who was partially paralyzed, was getting ready to *davven* and his daughter held up a mirror in front of him so that he could see if his *t'fillin* were placed properly. He looked and said, *Ot-dos bin ikh a davvener.* This is who I am. I'm a davvener; now I'm ready to *davven.* You see, we have to check out what might be obstructing our way before we enter the *davvenen.*

Show me a person today who doesn't have 'distracting thoughts' about important things that they have to do while *davvenen*. In the middle of *davvenen*, I might remember, *"Oy!* I have to call" so and so, "they are sitting *shiv'ah."* Or, "I have to put the *hallah* in the oven."

Once, Reb Levi Yitzhak of Berditchev walked over to a couple of Hasidim after *Minhah* and shakes their hands, saying, *"Shalom Aleikhem."** So one of them says: "Why are you giving us a *shalom aleikhem?* We've been here the whole time and greeted you earlier." "No-o-o-o," he says, "When you were *davvenen Sh'monei Essreh*, you were traveling in Odessa!"

If I said, "I don't want to deal with those 'distracting thoughts' right now, I'll remember what I have to remember later," the thoughts would insist on being heard. They would "That's what you always say, and you never remember." So, on weekdays, I keep a little pad of paper next to me while I *davven*; you should see how many important things I remember in the middle of the *davvenen*. By the time I have finished *davvenen*, I may have a nice to-do list for the day, but thoughts didn't succeed in distracting me for longer than it took to write them down. They weren't able to persist, and that is important.

A lot of *davvenen* has to do with attunement. The hardest instrument in the whole orchestra to tune is the oboe. All the others you can tune and adjust. But the orchestra first tunes up when the oboe plays the A, which the violins take over, and then everyone else tunes into that. Having tuned in, then they will be able to play together in harmony. The question is, if I just come from having been on the computer, and taking care of some business, that mind is not the best mind for *davvenen*. I have to re-tune myself, the same way that I would have to re-tune an instrument.

What is the best way to do that? There is something our distant cousins, the Christian monks call *lectio divina*.

---

* Rabbi Levi Yitzhak of Berditchev (1740-1809), one of the most beloved of all Hasidic masters. See my book with Netanel Miles-Yepez, *A Merciful God: Stories and Teachings of the Holy Rebbe, Levi Yitzhak of Berditchev.*

They take a sacred text, like we study Torah, and read and contemplate that text prior to prayer. That's why, for instance, when I was in the *yeshivah,* we would study *hasidus* for a while before *davvenen* and then meditate on it. In other words, we bring it to ourselves and say, "Now all my apertures are open to these vibrations in the *davvenen* field, and not in the business field, or the traffic field." That is also important.

I read a paragraph or two of something that inspires me and, of course, that does it right away. It attunes me in the same way my eyes focus on something and adjust for varying degrees of light. In the same way, I read something inspirational, and there is an accommodation of my awareness to it.

It is also important to make a list of items you want to bring into prayer, and the people you want to pray for. Let me spend some time on that. There are some people, who are really into 'spirituality,' and who have the sense that now they're doing their 'practice.' I'm making fun of that, because that means that it is all about them, and never stops being about them. On the other hand, when I'm about to *davven,* if I want to really have a sense that I'm not speaking to the wall, I need to bring a real need to God from time to time.

As I discussed before, there is a scriptural commandment to *davven,* which is separate from the *siddur,* and comes from the heart, and then there is the rabbinic commandment to recite the words prescribed by the Sages. But if I don't have that moment when I can say in my prayers: "Dear God, today I need little bit more energy; I need to be a good instrument in Your hand, and to have a clear head. I also have some concerns for one of my sons, so please, *Ribbono shel Olam,* You're also father, please take care of that." Do you see what I'm saying? When I can get into a place, it's all real for me. Then when I get into parts of the service that deal with these matters, it makes a difference to me. I have already said that this is for real for me. So make a list of all the things you want to pray for.

Before there were PDAs, Personal Digital Assistants, I used to have a little set of 3 x 5 cards, with rubrics from the *Sh'monei Essreh* written on them. I would have awareness, *t'shuvah*, forgiveness, energy, and healing. If, during the day, it occurred to me that there was something around one of these that I needed to do, then I would take that card out and make a little mark on it. Then when I started to *davven,* especially the *Sh'monei Essreh,* I would be able to say, "And please heal" so-and-so at this point.

Nebbukh, recently, the son of a friend of mine was killed in an automobile accident, and just today they got up from *shiv'ah.* So what is my prayer? First of all, I pray for the consolation of the family; but even more for that soul to find her way, to be able to reach out to those beings who are there to help, to give an orientation to that soul. I can think of several other people like, Shalva Rochel, who passed on recently; they too are in my prayer at that point.

Sometimes you can say *Kaddish,* and sometimes you can't. What is more important is to send a 'care packages' for them. What's a care package? When you say, *"El Male rahamim,* "God, full of mercy, grant perfect repose and rest for the soul" of so-and-so. Then it says, "Because we are going to give some *tzedakah* in order to remember that soul." Now what does that mean? There is, according to our teaching, no realm in the whole order of creation, where one can do as much as you can do in this world of *Assiyah,* the doing world. When you come to the other world, you have the reward of what you have done here, but you can't add anything. So whenever we study Torah, we send the merit up to the person who taught us, or we give *tzedakah* and send the merit up in someone's memory; we increase the merit for them. That's why I call it sending 'care packages.'

How do I launder money? I turn it into *tzedakah,* and then I can I collect it *up there.* I'm just using this as a *mashal.*

When you have people whom you love, and you have pictures of them in an album, and you show the pictures to someone, and the person looks at them with some kind of interest, it creates a good feeling in you. They say: "Oh, how wonderful; these are your grand-children?" Something happened just because you had an album. In Brooklyn, many Orthodox children have Rebbe cards they collect, cards with the pictures of different Rosh Yeshivahs, of Hasidic Rebbes, and the kids trade them: "I'll give you a Hazon Ish for two Hafetz Hayy-ims."

When you think of someone who did something holy, something beautiful, something heroic, or who taught something nice, and you can connect yourself with them, that's a wonderful thing to do. When it is a *yahrzeit,* you do that; but you can do it even if it's not a *yahrzeit.* It doesn't have to be someone Jewish. I think if I were to see Woody Guthrie singing one of those labor songs, that that would get me into *davvenen,* too. This is part attune-ment beforehand.

More important than what you bring in that moment from outside is what you already remember from before. For instance, do you remember a highlight from last Rosh Hashanah? If you do, then you can tune into that high-light and easily bring it into your *davvenen.* In this way, you are much better prepared to *davven* than those who cannot.

That's why a *niggun* is so important. There is a beauti-ful song by Reb Levi Yitzhak of Berditchev that begins: "*Ribbono shel Olam,* I want to sing You a *You-song,* a *Thou-song.* To the East is You; to the West is You . . ." Even the words *Ribbono shel Olam* are in this melody are so power-ful. Reb Dovid'l Zeller, of blessed memory, would sit with people and chant that for a long time.* The idea was not to bring God *here,* because God is already here, but to make myself present to God. You sing that phrase, *Ribbono Shel Olam,* and then you say, "Now I want to say part of *Shaharit* for You," and you begin with that. What a difference it makes!

You also need to decide what highlights you need to touch upon this time in prayer. When you look at the four levels of the service, you begin with the body and the *b'rakhot* of the body; the blessings for the sight of the eyes and the use of the body. Some days you need more of that, and you say with *kavvanah, Ha'noteyn l'ya'ef ko'ah,* "Give me the energy." You'll say the rest of it too, but that's where you want to fill the tank that day.

Another place you might highlight is: "I cried out to You, and You healed me when I was sick. I really want to give You thanks for that; it feels is so much better not to be sick." You might say the rest of it, but that's the highlight for you.

Or you may come to the place before the *Sh'ma'* and say, "My heart has been so ripped apart; part of me wants to be here, part of me wants to be there, and I wish that my heart would just come together. Unify my heart, put my heart together so it shouldn't be so broken into different pieces."

It's good before the *davvenen* to be really deliberate about this, and to say, "Today I need to pay attention to these particular highlights."

Another thing I shouldn't say, but I'll say it anyway: decide what you are going to skip on the days when you don't have time for the whole thing. If you don't decide beforehand, you'll feel a lot of pressure to finish it all, or you'll skip in an uneven way. Better a little bit with real

---

* Rabbi David Zeller (1946-2007) was a much loved musician and teacher, and the author of *The Soul of the Story.*

intention, real *kavvanah*, than a whole lot without *kavvanah*.

Nevertheless, make sure that you leave time for the end. What do I mean? I have mentioned a number times now that people often 'hang up the phone' too soon when they are waiting for answers. During *yeridat ha'shefa*, when you are coming down the mountain of prayer, it is important to collect what you discovered on the way up. That's where you get your action directives for the day, from these moments of inspiration.

People think that prophecy is like sitting in front of the prophecy machine waiting for the message from God to come through. Just pay attention the insights you get in your *davvenen*, and throughout your day. How else is it going to come, if not in the midst of your life? Just be open to receiving it, and try to apply it.

One of the difficult issues to deal with has to do with the psychological reinforcement. When I do something well and reward myself, I reinforce it and it becomes stronger in me. So when you are ready to come down from the *davvenen*, and you remember the places where you got your 'prophecy,' as it were, and you bring that down with you, then you get closer to *a guided life*. That is why we reinforce intuitions with sensation, feeling, and reason, because we can do something with all of these; intuition is not so much under our control.

What am I going to do to reinforce intuition? I can't give it a reward like giving a dog a bone. There is only one thing I can do: *I can take it more seriously.* The more I say to intuition, "You're right, you're right," the more refined it will become, and more will come through it. And that, when it is tied to prayer, leads to a guided life.

The Charity Box

As you pray, you should also have a *pushke*, or a *tzedakah* box next to you. There are some people who say:

"I give so much *tzedakah*. Let me write out the check once and for all, and give it away." The RaMBaM, Maimonides, had a conversation going about this: Is it better that you should give a lump sum, or is it better that you should give little by little? He says it is better to give little by little because you increase the *mitzvah* with your action. You are always there in it.*

I have five *pushkes* in my *davvenen* room, and on different occasions, I put some money into each one of them. There is a phrase in the *davvenen* that says, "You, *Adonai*, You created the heavens and the heavens of heavens and everything else." It goes on to say, "And you invigorate them all." That's the time to drop something into the *pushke*. That's been a custom— *V'attah m'hayyeh et kulam*, "And you invigorate them all."

When you go to *shul* on Thursday mornings, you'll see people putting money in the *tzedakah* box. It is a 'put up or shut up' thing.

Teachers and Prayer Partners

Before the Ba'al Shem Tov passed on, some of his disciples asked him, "To whom should we go when you are gone? Who will be our next leader? How will we know him? He said, "If you ask someone, 'How do you get rid of pride?' and they answer with a prescription, that person is not your *rebbe*. With that you have to struggle to your dying moment." In fact, the last words that the Ba'al Shem Tov were, *Al t'vi'eni regel ga'ava*, "Don't lead me to the foot of pride." Can you imagine how the Ba'al Shem Tov must have looked back over his entire life at that last moment, playing it all back? He looks back at the big wake he has left behind, at how many people are going to follow in his footsteps; shouldn't he take some pride in that at that moment? So he is saying, "Please, *Ribbono shel*

---

* Rabbi Moshe ben Maimon (1135-1204), better known as Maimonides, was a great Spanish legal authority and philosopher.

Olam, this is really hard; take that temptation to pride from me." Then he said something else to his Hasidim: "I want you to sing the *niggun* that Reb Mikheleh Zlotchover composed, and I promise you, that wherever you are going be, whatever you are going to do, if you need a prayer partner, I'll join you and pray for whatever your intention is in prayer." So that is a good *niggun* for you to know.

When my *rebbe*, Reb Yosef Yitzhak Schneersohn was about to pass on, he sent us a teaching that began with the words, *Bati l'gani ahoti kallah,* "I came into my garden . . ." If you talk to Habadnikes, they will all know different ent versions of this teaching, because every year afterward, the Rebbe, Reb Menachem Mendel Schneerson take another paragraph and elucidate it. Many, many years ago, I took the key words from that teaching and added them to Reb Mikheleh Zlotchover's melody so that I could log-on to both the Ba'al Shem Tov and my *rebbe* (as prayer partners) at the same time:

I came to my garden,
From beyond time and space,
To meet my bride, my beloved,
At our special meeting place,
For not the angels of heaven above,
But You, my souls I love.

My Lord, My Love, My Groom,
With Thee let me commune;
Please regard
That in my heart
For Thee I have made a room.

My Lord, My Love, My Groom,
Please save me from doom,
I shall heed
Thy word in deed
In joy but never in gloom.

Save my soul from evil's rule,
It makes one act just like a fool;
So that the truth I'll realize
And follow Thee, Oh Eternally wise.

To see then clear, just how ideal
It is for me, Thee near to feel
So hear my Lord, do hear my sigh
With Torah, Turning, and Right acts
To Thee my knot I tie.

It is a very deep thing and always gets to me. When you put it together with those words, it is very strong. For right now, I want to ask the Ba'al Shem Tov to pray, be my prayer partner, that these teachings should truly benefit people in their *davven*. To that, let me say, *Amen*.

Thank you holy Ba'al Shem.

Exiting the Davvenen

When you come down from the *davvenen*, and exit it with your insights in hand, don't forget to put some money into the *tzedakah* box in gratitude. Then, if it is morning, you should you take your *tallit* and *t'fillin* and put them together lovingly. It is so important to sing something happy at this point. Most of the time, we simply rush away. But you should take the time to fold the *tallit* carefully and to put the *t'fillin* away. If you do it mechanically, you can get done fast, okay, but you could also sing something at that time. It helps you to get into that field of *simhah*, joy and gratitude for what you have just been doing. Then as you sit down to breakfast, you get the sense of how God is nourishing you. We forget that so easily, so quickly. "Oh, thank you, *Ribbono shel Olam*, what a good breakfast You have provided me!"

Reb Zushe of Anipol would never ask people for food. He would say out loud, "Oh, *Ribbono shel Olam*, Zushe is hungry!" And when someone would bring him some food, he would say, "Oh, thank You *God* for making sure that Zushe should have something to eat!" That attitude translates into a lot of good feeling for the rest of the day, and gives a lot of *simhah* to being a good Jew.

Question and Answer Session

Question: I'm really appreciating what you said about the morning practice and how it goes into the day. I am thinking about that as kind of springtime and a beginning. For me, it's the most important thing to hear about. I'm also wondering if you could say something about an evening practice, or something later before you go to sleep, or even during the day.

Reb Zalman: I want to say something about *Minhah* in the middle of the day. Do you remember phone booths? When I would come into in New York on the Grand Central, and it would be time *davven Minhah*, sometimes I would step into a telephone booth and pick up the receiver and start *davvenen*. It wasn't something I was comfortable doing in the middle of the station, but the telephone booth made it comfortable for me. The point is, whatever it takes, this is an important daily prayer.

The afternoon prayer is short and abrupt, just one chapter of the Psalms, *Ashrey*, and the *Amidah*. It is fast, but it can also be crucial. Imagine you are in middle of some important business at work, and someone you love very much calls you. You can't take much time out from what you are doing to talk, but at the same time, you don't want to talk to your beloved even for a moment in business language. So a nice switch happens, you say, "Listen honey, I really want to talk to you, but I don't have time right now. I'm in the middle of some business, but I'll call you later, okay?" Do you see what I'm saying? *Minhah* is that kind of 'interruption,' where we say, "*Ribbono shel Olam*, I'm in the middle of my day, a crazy day, and I'm in a telephone booth, but I just wanted to tell You I love you with a quick *Ashrey and Amidah.*" Or you might send up a few 'arrow prayers' at that time as well.

Question: Did you say, "arrow prayers"?

Reb Zalman: Yes, arrow prayers. Jacob says, "I captured the land with my sword and my bow."* And the *Targum* translates that metaphorically as, *Beharbiy uvkashtiy,* "with my prayer and my entreaty." In other words, the weapon of a Jew is prayer. When you send up a quick, momentary awareness, saying, "Dear God, I need your help" . . . "Dear God, I know You're there" . . . "Dear God, I'm in the middle of things and I'm busy, but I love You." These are called 'arrow prayers' because they don't take very long, and they go directly to the heart of God.

---

* Genesis 48:22.

Twelfth Talk
A Dialogue on Davvenology

Reb Michael: We now live in a desert of people disconnected from God, some of whom want to be connected, and want to observe Judaism, and don't know how. As I see it, Judaism as a whole needs to undergo a positive transformation, like the one you have made with Jewish Renewal, but how do we begin to connect people?

Reb Zalman: Jewish Renewal came about with the understanding of paradigm shift. What we were criticizing belonged to the old paradigm. In that paradigm, we would say on our holy days? "The *goyim* had it in for us; we fought them; God helped us and we won; and now we eat." But in the new paradigm, we have moved away from that kind of triumphalism.

What is most troubling with radical Islam today, with right-wing Christianity, and our own fundamentalists, is simply that all of them say: "In the end, *we* will win and be justified; everyone else will either be with us, or they go to hell." But if I go to an organic view of our global connection, in which all of us are seen as organically connected, it is a whole different ballgame.

Reb Michael: But most people are connected and don't know it.

Reb Zalman: When you are organic, some of it is more conscious, some of it is less conscious. For instance: my bone marrow has a consciousness that produces red blood cells, but at the same time, it doesn't have the same consciousness that my brain has. We are not all as conscious of the connection as others. Nor does everything have to be verbally connected. Some awareness is inherent in the nonverbal somatic consciousness. If I were to look at the bell shaped curve, and if I were to take all of me and look at the distribution along the curve, I would see that the higher awareness of my body is located in Sigma 2 plus. That awareness is a little bit aware; the rest of is unaware, and so it is with every community. There are some people who are unaware. What is important is for people who are aware to *stay in their awareness* because this will infect other people.

Reb Michael: Maybe it *will* infect the rest of the people. What I am concerned about is that an awareness of God has to be brought in. Doing the rituals alone, without that awareness, does not guarantee a real contact.

Reb Zalman: That is true. In order to bring about awareness of God, it is the same situation. Some people will do the ritual only; some people will say that they can be aware of God without ritual; but it is the people who will do ritual with awareness who will influence both sides.

Reb Michael: My concern is that with this paradigm shift, and the break from the old-school, Ashkenazi and Sefardi Judaism, we also had a break in the continuity of the mental consciousness *gestalt* that connects us. How can that be reestablished?

Reb Zalman: You are taking the role of the pessimist, and I am taking the role of the optimist for the sake of this conversation.

Reb Michael: In reality, I'm optimistic.

194

Reb Zalman: When I start looking at what has happened in the publication of Jewish media at this point—never before in history has there been such a plethora of Jewish material.

Recently, I got a note from someone reading the work of Avraham Maimonides, Maimonides' son, and he is aware that the son differs from his father.* So he asked me whether this word *ma'avak*, which he mentions in his book, in this struggle with one's lower nature, is the same as the Arabic *jihad*. Now this is from a *yeshivah bokher*. When I see more and more material like this becoming available, and more and more people becoming aware of it, I am greatly encouraged. It is always the *avant-garde* that is at first in disrepute. There are now some people in New York who have been refugees from the closed Hasidic ghettoes of Brooklyn. Those folks are in disrepute among the people of their home base, but out of that soil will grow that which you are hoping for.

Reb Michael: That would be good.

Reb Zalman: There were a couple of other things that we wanted to bring in here.

Reb Michael: To scrutinize one's motives under the moral microscope for authenticity and honesty, and how they fit into one's understanding reality, and one's awareness of God.

Reb Zalman: Here is something so amazing to me. There is a man by the name Alan Morinis who has been traveling across the country. He has been infected by *mussar*,

---

* Rabbi Avraham ben Moshe Maimuni (1186-1237), the son of Maimonides and leader of the Egyptian Jews who practiced a form of Jewish Sufism.

Jewish ethical behavior, and he is speaking to people about *mussar*. *Mussar* shows itself in Torah, *avodah,* and *gemillut hassadim*. It shows itself first and foremost in *gemillut hassadim* because how do we give our *tzedakah*? And are we giving it with the right motives? When it comes to prayer, the question is always authenticity. How much are you doing it to show off? How much are you doing in order to be socially acceptable in that that particular circle of people? Morinis is asking the question: Are you aware that your praying is in the presence of God? It is also important to study Torah sensing the presence of God both in the text and in the mind.

There was a story of one of the rebbes who, before he started to learn each day, would recite: "To the wicked one, God said, What business have you got to speak of my law?" This was his way of saying that he would do *t'shuvah* before studying in order to get himself into the Presence. His intention was, "I am studying Your mind, Your will, and Your wisdom."

I think much good is happening now, little by little, and at the same time, the old institutions are breaking down.

Reb Michael: What comes to me now is that many people, many Jews and Catholics have an accounting system: *I am doing the* mitzvot, *and gaining points, so I will get into the World-to-Come.*

Reb Zalman: That is what Rabbi Emanuel Rackman so beautifully pointed out when he said that people are trying to be *yotze',* having "extricated themselves from the grasp of obligation."* I have done it. I have deposited my merits in the Bank of Heaven, and now I am free of the burden of the commandment. That is where Hasidism

---

* *Yotze':* having fulfilled the law's demand, I am now free and out of the reach of the obligation.

and the New Hasidism of the fourth turning is asking: How does it transform a human being? That has been your question all along.

Reb Michael: Does it transform us? What does it do to you internally, in your life? So the way I see it, it has to be done with the right motives and the right attitude.

Reb Zalman: Now the question is, how do we infuse it into people? That is not an easy thing.

There is a wonderful teaching of the Ba'al Shem Tov about Moses at the burning bush. God tells Moses: "Take the shoes off your feet, you are standing on holy ground."* In Hasidic parlance, "Take the shoes off your feet" is interpreted to mean "Take the lock off your habits." Only when you are free of your habits can you be in the here and now, can you be in the presence of the living God.

Reb Michael: I still sense a conflict: *This is the* right *way to* davven. *You should do it at* these *times, and say* these *words, and have the* right *attitude; but you still have to take the lock off your habits.*

Reb Zalman: I was talking with a young *baal t'shuvah.* When I asked him about his prayer life, he said he was doing it all according to the *siddur,* but the most important part comes for him when he is doing *hitbodedut.* Then he speaks to God in English, directly. That is wonderful. So he got that from Reb Nahman. I then pointed something out to him: when he is *davvenen* from the *siddur* in Hebrew, he is fulfilling a rabbinic command, but when he asking God for what he needs, he is fulfilling the scriptural command. Then I told him that my rebbe's fa-

---

* Exodus 3:5.

197

ther, Reb Sholem Dov Baer of Lubavitch,* pointed out that if you *davven* the regular *davvenen* in the *siddur* and the particular prayer touches you and it is like *hitbodedut,* taking it personally—like *Ahavat Olam Ahavtanu,* "Please have pity on me and in the abundance of Your compassion help me and lead me in the right path"—then the rabbinic prayer, having become something personal, takes on the form of a scriptural commandment, because you mean it for yourself. This is called *ada'ata d'nafshey,* to pray with self-involvement.

Reb Michael: So it seems that what's important here is to strive for a relationship with God, and that needs to be paramount.

Reb Zalman: How do you speak about a relationship with God? You call it a 'covenant with God.' Most people don't pay attention to the word covenant anymore—that this is a relationship that has to be vital; it is not to be broken and constantly renewed; every day it is fresh and has to be reaffirmed and renewed.

Reb Michael: In my experience, people find it difficult to appeal to God, saying, "This is what I need."

Reb Zalman: But it also is necessary to be able to *kvetch.* Yet before you do, it is important to say, "I am so aware of Your constant generosity keeping us all alive, and Your willingness to make sure that we should live heavenly days right here on this earth; because of that, I have the *hutzpah* to ask You to help us with this and that."

Rabbi Levi Yitzhak of Berditchev asks—What right have we to make the *b'rakhah Hannun Ha'marbeh Lislo'ah,* that God will forgive us? That You are always forgiving

---

* Rabbi Shalom Dov Baer Schneersohn of Lubavitch (1860-1920), the fifth Lubavitcher Rebbe.

us. How do I know? So he puts it this way: A child wants to eat an apple. The father says: "You will get the apple after dinner; not now." So the child starts reciting the blessing over the fruit. What can the father do? He doesn't want the child to make a blessing in vain, so he gives him the apple. So too, when we make the blessing, God has to forgive us. There is a relationship, that family relationship that we have with our God that is absent in other religions.

How do we sustain a commitment to seek in the presence of God? This is an important one. Let us go and check this out. I really do have a sense that when we are in connection, we feel it in a way; that is what *d'veikut* is. Sometimes the *d'veikut* is more manifest, and we feel the grace of God surrounding us. Sometimes the *d'veikut* shows in a certain sense of absence and longing. I understand that when I feel the longing for God, it means that God is longing for me too. I get to reciting the Song of Songs and say: "On my bed at night I sought the One whom my heart loves. I sought Him and found Him not."*

In my life, I have experienced times of longing that have brought me so much closer to God then when I was relaxed in the presence of God.

Reb Michael: This is interesting from my perspective, because this is one of the ways to bring God in.

Reb Zalman: One of the problems that I am trying to address in this series is for people to *davven* during the week. If you don't *davven* during the week, you are not in the process of living with God. Remember when I spoke of dawn and dusk? These are special times when we have the double consciousness of day and night. It is so

---

* Song of Songs 3:1.

much easier to pray at that time, and when we do that, we nurture the connection we have with God.

Reb Michael: The way I see it, we need to have a practice every day; preferably more than once in the day. With everything we do, we need to remember God; otherwise, we drift.

Reb Zalman: It is said, a *tzaddik* is one who makes 100 blessings a day. But you don't make a blessing ostentatiously, to show how religious you are. You say it quietly with a wink at God. In the morning, you say, "For every breath I thank You." This is what entrainment in the traditional ritual *can* bring—notice that I didn't say *does* bring your. When a *b'rakhah* is made with consciousness, it works.

I want to say something about how we understand the love of God, even when we aren't feeling the presence of God. When we send up an arrow prayer, saying: "God, are you there? Look inside of me. See me; I'm open to You. I'm transparent to You." In that moment, we are connected to God, precisely because we weren't feeling the presence. We are connected by our love and longing.

That's why I have that little bell in my car, so it should ring every time I hit a pothole, and remind me of all that is not visible, to remind me of my love. But the blessings in arrow prayers have to be done by conscious repetition. We must stay aware that this also how reality exists for us.

I also want to return to the subject of *meditating Jews* and *Jewish meditation.* As I said before, people package things as 'Jewish meditation,' which turn out to be Buddhist meditation with a little Jewish input, like a Hebrew word, a phrase, or a chant. It is not a meditation rooted in the Torah, as we have with: "Know you therefore today and put the knowledge in the heart." Jewish meditation is what makes us know it and put it into the heart. That's why I have said so much about steering the mind, and moving from the 'ought' to the 'is.'

Most people today talk about meditation as if it came from the East. But in Psalm 19:15, we have: "May the words of my mouth and the meditation of my heart be acceptable in Your sight, O Lord, my Rock and my Redeemer." In Psalm 8:4-5, we have, "When I see the heavens, the work of Your fingers . . . I say, Who is man that you be mindful of him?" This is a guide to contemplation. That's why it's so important to recognize the way in which Scripture leads us to work with our consciousness in the mind and in the heart.

This is our meditation, but it is also found in Christianity.

Back in 1946, when I was still a card-carrying Lubavitcher Hasid, teaching in our *yeshivah* in New Haven, Connecticut, I wanted to get some books on psychology in order to be a better teacher. So I went to the library and happened upon a couple of books on a table marked "New Acquisitions." One of these books was called *Difficulties in Mental Prayer* by Father Eugene Boylan, a Trappist monk. When I saw this book I was shocked. For all I knew, only Lubavitchers were involved in anything that I would call "mental prayer." Even other Hasidic groups only dealt with vocal prayer—never *hitbonenut*, mental prayer. With great eagerness, I picked up the book and I saw that he was describing the same troubles that we have: trying to stick with our intention in *davvenen*; not being distracted when unwanted ideas are popping up; and bringing the desired thoughts into the heart.

From there, I went on to read about the Ignatian method of meditation, and I saw that this doesn't require hours and hours—just 15 or 20 minutes at most, and this makes a real shift.* That, by the way, is the way in which meditation has to go nowadays.

Reb Michael: Can you describe this method?

Reb Zalman: The first thing is the meditation of place. Am I now in the presence of God? Am I in touch with God's will for me and for the world and what I have to do? What are the obstacles to fulfilling that? I hold this up to God in prayer that the obstacles be removed from me. I see how important my actions will be, and what the consequences and the fruits of the actions are going to be in the long run. I see myself as an agent of the living God in what I am doing in the world. There is another standard, the standard of evil, the standard of the world, and I want to say, "No, this is not my standard." I place myself in God's camp.

When someone asked him: "Ignatius, what will you do if the Pope outlaws your Jesuits?" He said, "After 15 minutes in the oratory with God and it will be all the same to me." Just let me pray for 15 minutes and I can handle it. He wasn't saying that it wouldn't make a difference. It makes a difference; he'd be hurt, and his life work would have been destroyed; but after 15 minutes in the presence of God he believed he would be able to handle it.

I think this kind of meditation is what we need in our busy lives today. All the other methods that take a long time are not for our present circumstances.

Some things that have to do with the kind of consciousness you need to fulfill the commandments. There are some people who will say, "I'm fulfilling my obligation; I don't need to do all this spirituality that you guys

---

* Ignatius of Loyola (1491-1556) was a Spanish knight, priest, and founder of the Jesuit order of priests.

202

are peddling." But I say, "All right, then, let me ask you a question: Imagine you are tying *tzitzit* onto a *tallit*, and you are not stating that you're doing this *l'shem mitzvat tzitzit* with the express intention that these *tzitzit* be used to fulfill the *mitzvah* of *tzitzit*. Will the *tzitzit* be kosher?" Only with the intention will they be kosher.

If you want to eat *matzot* on first night of Pesah, you have to be baking the *matzot l'shem matzot mitzvah* or else they do not fulfill the obligation. So intention and consciousness are very important. Even writing a *gett* for a divorce proceeding has to be done *lishmo, lishmah,* and *l'shem gerushin* with the intention focused on this man, this woman, and with the intention to be a legal instrument for the divorce.

In studying Torah you need the *intention* to study Torah *lishmah*, which is to say *for the sake of the soul, for the sake of the Torah, for the sake of the Shekhinah.* All halakhic authorities agree that *mitzvot* demand the consciousness of intentionality. It is not that they should stop doing what they're doing, but that they should also track their awareness.

Before we say *L'shem Yihud Kudsha b'rikh hu ush'khinteh*—which states that "I am doing this for the sake of the union of the Holy One, blessed be He, and the Divine Presence," and behold I am making myself fully present in this particular holy act—what do you need to do? It is in an interior act, a visualization. See yourself in your bodily imagination going through this in the highest possible. If I am about to count *sefirat ha'omer*, I go inside and I see myself going doing this *mitzvah*, feeling the texture of each day, seeing myself climbing the ladder up to God, and receiving the grace that is coming down for this day for good. I've tasted this and I'm doing it already, and then I start saying the *b'rakhah*, and then all this intention enters into the *b'rakhah*. The Rabbis of the Talmud said: *Mahshavah tovah ha'kadosh barukh hu m'tzar'fah l'ma'asseh,* "The Holy One, blessed be He, takes good thoughts and connects them to action." In this way, a *mitzvah* is completed holistically.

But *mahshavah* means more than mere thought. It means scheming, weaving together on the level of reason, and the level of feeling, and the level of intuition; it is feeling it in your body then when you actually do that kind of thinking; it is connected to the *mitzvah*.

Michael, what else would you say is important to talk about today?

Reb Michael: I believe it is important that we get rid of all concepts of what God is. Holding a concept of God is a form of idolatry, and very dangerous.

Reb Zalman: How do you propose people to that?

Reb Michael: It is very simple, you ask God, "How can I get rid of my concepts so that I can know You."

Reb Zalman: I once heard something from Jean Houston that was very helpful to me. She was talking about peoples' mantras. I'm not talking about the mantras you recite with your mouths that are part of *mantra japa*. She was talking about the mantras that are going on in your head all the time: *I am a this; I am a that; I'm a this; I'm a that; I think this; I think that.* I have a whole bunch of these recordings that I'm constantly running, and there's no way to get rid of them except by recording over them with a stronger *mantra*. That's what I'm saying is part of that meditative process,to be able to say: *Ana avda d'kudsha brikh hu*, "I'm a servant of the Holy One, blessed be He." I am a part of living Earth, I am a part of God in this body. All these affirmations that you can make are the ones that make the difference, because by this, the other affirmations get pushed away.

Reb Michael: This brings to mind Rabbi Kalonymus Kalmish Shapira of Piasetzno, who pointed out that it is very important to form "conscious communities."* They do not have to be *frum,* but they have to be where people get together and practice and reinforce each other.

Reb Zalman: As the prophet says, when the people talk to one another, God listens in and writes it into His book of memories. This interests God more than anything else that happens, the dialogue of the devout.

All the blessings to you!

---

* Kalonymus Kalman Shapira, *Conscious Community: A Guide to Inner Work,* translated by Andrea Cohen-Kiener.

Biographies

Zalman Schachter-Shalomi, better known as 'Reb Zalman,' was born in Zholkiew, Poland, in 1924. His family fled the Nazi oppression in 1938 and finally landed in New York City in 1941. Descended from a distinguished family of Belzer Hasidim, he became a HaBaD Hasid as a teenager while still living in Antwerp, Belgium. He was later ordained by HaBaD-Lubavitch in 1947 and became one of the Lubavitcher Rebbe's first generation of outreach workers. He later earned his MA in psychology from Boston University in 1956 and a DHL from Hebrew Union College in 1968. He is professor emeritus of Psychology of Religion and Jewish Mysticism at Temple University and is World Wisdom Chair holder emeritus at Naropa University. Today he is primarily known as the Rebbe and father of the neo-Hasidic Jewish Renewal movement and is widely considered one of the world's foremost authorities on Hasidism and Kabbalah. He is the author of *Spiritual Intimacy: A Study of Counseling in Hasidism* (1991), *Jewish with Feeling: Guide to a Meaningful Jewish Practice* (2005), co-author of *A Heart Afire: Stories and Teachings of the Early Hasidic Masters* (2009). Reb Zalman currently lives in Boulder, Colorado.

Michael Kosacoff, is a spiritual teacher, psychologist, and filmmaker living in Boulder, Colorado.

8436340R0

Made in the USA
Charleston, SC
09 June 2011